What Model for
Europe?

What Model for Europe?

Michael Emerson
with André Dramais

The MIT Press
Cambridge, Massachusetts
London, England

This book was set in Palatino by Asco Trade Typesetting Ltd., Hong Kong, and printed and bound by Halliday Lithograph in the United States of America.

Library of Congress Cataloging-in-Publication Data

Emerson, Michael.
    What model for Europe?

    Bibliography: p.
    Includes index.
    1. Labor policy—European Economic Community countries.
2. European Economic Community countries—Social policy.
3. Industrial relations—European Economic Community countries.
4. Social security—European Economic Community countries.
I. Dramais, André.   II. Title.
HD8380.5.E47   1988   331.11′094   87-15151
ISBN 0-262-05036-6
ISBN 0-262-55016-4 (pbk.)

To Barbara, Sophie, Tom,
and Lucie

.

Contents

Tables   ix

Acknowledgments   xiii

1 Introduction: The Search for a European Model   1

**2 Theoretical Models for Employment and Social
Policies   5**
2.1 Competitive Models of Neoclassical Inspiration   6
2.2 Efficiency Models of Wage Rigidity and Employment
Security   8
2.3 Political Models of Neocorporatist Inspiration   13
2.4 Some Eclectic Contributions from Mainstream
Macroeconomics   20

**3 Core Features of the Socioeconomic Model in
Practice   25**
3.1 Pay Systems   25
3.2 Hiring and Firing Regulations   32
3.3 Income Maintenance for Those of Working Age   39
3.4 Basic Social Services   52
3.5 Poverty and Income Redistribution: The Overall
Results   65

4 Return to a High-Employment Society 73

4.1 The Trap 73

4.2 Springing the Trap 77

4.3 Concluding Remarks 85

Appendix A Social Security Systems in the Industrialized Countries 89

Appendix B Econometric Model Simulation of a Medium-Term Scenario for a Reduction of Unemployment in the European Community 117
André Dramais

References 141

Index 149

Tables

3.1 Measures of short- and long-run real wage rigidity 27

3.2 Absenteeism from work because of ill-health 42

3.3 Number of beneficiaries of disability pensions 43

3.4 Invalidity, disability, and work injury benefits 45

3.5 Family and maternity benefits 48

3.6 Share of social expenditures in 1981 54

3.7 Replacement rates of social security old-age pensions for workers with average wages in manufacturing, for couples, 1969–1980 60

3.8 Projections of the share of elderly in the population and pensions expenditure on unchanged policies 61

3.9 Projections of pensions expenditure on unchanged and changed policies 62

3.10 Pre- and posttransfer poverty rates in 1979 67

3.11 Change in income distribution in the United States from 1980 to 1984 as a result of changes in taxation and transfer payment programs 70

4.1 Breakdown of the increase in social benefits in eight European Community countries between 1970 and 1983 76

4.2 Social security contributions in 1983 78

4.3 Summary of a high-employment society in the European Community 79

A.1 Unemployment benefits in 1985 90

A.2   Sickness and maternity benefits in 1985   91

A.3   Old-age pension benefits (public) in 1985   92

A.4   Invalidity and disability benefits in 1985   93

A.5   Family and income-maintenance benefits in 1985   94

A.6   Health care benefits (public) in 1985   95

A.7   Main features of various benefits for the United States,
       1961–1985   96

A.8   Main features of various benefits for Japan,
       1961–1985   97

A.9   Main features of various benefits for France,
       1961–1985   98

A.10   Main features of various benefits for Germany,
       1961–1985   99

A.11   Main features of various benefits for Italy,
       1961–1985   100

A.12   Main features of various benefits for the United
       Kingdom, 1961–1985   101

A.13   Main features of various benefits for Belgium,
       1961–1985   103

A.14   Main features of various benefits for the Netherlands,
       1961–1985   104

A.15   Main features of various benefits for Denmark,
       1961–1985   105

A.16   Main features of various benefits for Finland,
       1961–1985   106

A.17   Main features of various benefits for Norway,
       1961–1985   107

A.18   Main features of various benefits for Sweden,
       1961–1985   108

A.19   Main features of various benefits for Austria,
       1961–1985   109

A.20   Main features of various benefits for Switzerland,
       1961–1985   110

A.21   Main features of various benefits for Ireland,
       1961–1985   111

A.22   Main features of various benefits for Spain,
       1961–1985   112

A.23   Main features of various benefits for Greece,
       1961–1985   113

A.24   Main features of various benefits for Portugal,
       1961–1985   114

A.25   Evolution of public expenditures on social programs as
       percentage of GDP   115

B.1   Autonomous increase in public investment by 1% of
       baseline GDP, sustained over five years, for the
       European Community (ten countries)   124

B.2   Autonomous decrease in employers' social security
       contributions by 1% of baseline GDP, sustained over
       five years, for the European Community (ten
       countries)   126

B.3   Money supply expansion, with money supply growth
       kept autonomously one percentage point above the
       baseline nominal GDP growth for the European
       Community (ten countries)   128

B.4   Autonomous devaluation of the ECU by 10% with
       respect to baseline, sustained over five years, for the
       European Community (ten countries)   129

B.5   Nominal wages per employee kept 4% below baseline,
       over five years, without demand support, for the
       European Community (ten countries)   130

B.6   Nominal wages per employee kept 4% below baseline,
       over five years, with public expenditure increases
       sufficient to keep nominal GDP at baseline level for the
       European Community (ten countries)   131

B.7   Summary of growth strategy components   134

B.8   Main macroeconomic results for the baseline projection
       (B) and the employment-creating scenario (S) for the
       European Community (ten countries)   136

B.9   Labor market statistics for the baseline projection and
       scenario for the European Community (ten
       countries)   138

Acknowledgments

The present study was prepared during the 1985–1986 academic year when I was a Fellow at the Center for International Affairs at Harvard University, on leave from the Commission of the European Communities, Brussels. I am greatly indebted to many colleagues at the center for their help and encouragement, particularly Leslie Brown, Director of Fellows' Programme, and Susan Young. I am also grateful to L. Summers and J. Sachs of Harvard University, Department of Economics; M. Weitzman and O. Blanchard of MIT, Department of Economics; L. Rainwater of Harvard University, Department of Sociology; and the international policy staff of the US Social Security Administration, Washington, D.C.

What Model for Europe?

*Power and riches are enormous
and operose machines contrived
to produce a few trifling
conveniences to the body . . .
which, in spite of all our care,
are ready to burst into pieces
and crush in their ruins their
unfortunate possessor*
            Adam Smith, Theory of Moral Sentiments, pp. 182–183

1   Introduction:
The Search for a
European Model

At an international conference on technology and employment in Venice in early 1985, an American politician delivered a now familiar critique of the economic and social condition of Western Europe. To paraphrase: European unemployment is one of the Western world's major problems. It is due to manifold regulatory rigidities impeding job creation and to diminished economic incentives resulting from overblown social welfare programs. These rigidities need to be disposed of. He proceeded to explain the recipe behind the United States's considerable employment expansion. The American model was on offer. A European politician replied sharply: "You do not understand that Europe operates on a different model."

What model? Many people do have a vague idea about important differences in the economic and social models of Western Europe and the United States. Western Europe has much more social security and employment law. More difficult, however, is the definition of a normative European model, one that can be not only identified in custom and history but also justified by efficiency criteria. This would mean a model fully compatible with the political system's objectives, such as high and sustainable levels of employment, living standards, and equity in income distribution.

The economic and social model of a country or of an emerging block, such as the European Community, may be defined concretely in terms of three broad categories of public policy: (1) the regime for goods, services, and capital markets, (2) the regime for macroeconomic policy management, and (3) the regime for labor market and social policy.

Each of these categories deserves a book in itself. This study, however, is confined to labor market and social policy, for two reasons. First, whereas it would have been rewarding to attempt to cover all these main parts of the economic and social model, time has imposed a more selective approach. Second, it is principally in the third category that Europe's options are at present most unsettled.

As regards the other two categories the European Community's objectives are rather clear. The regime for goods, services, and capital markets is basically a free market one, with the European Community having adopted in 1985 an ambitious program to eliminate all remaining internal frontiers—physical, technical, and fiscal—by 1992. Much remains to be done to achieve this objective. But the program is clear, and the European Community has also made some changes in the voting rules of the Treaty of Rome in favor of majority voting in the Council of Ministers to expedite decision making in this area; this was done through the Single European Act, a new supplementary treaty whose ratification was completed in early 1987.

The regime for macroeconomic policy management is at present influenced by commitments, exemplified in the workings of the European monetary system, to monetary stabilization and economic policy convergence. Looking further ahead, the European Community has the objective of establishing a monetary union. This objective was confirmed in 1985 with its inscription into the Single European Act and thus for the first time into the treaties of the European Community. Pursuit of these macroeconomic integration goals can offer advantages to the economy in the nature of a more favorable environment for investment, for stabilization policy that should be able to achieve its objectives at less cost to the real economy, and, finally, for international economic policy that could be conducted with a stronger European bargaining power.

Turning to the third category, we try to evaluate whether or to what degree Western Europe's "advanced" labor and social security regimes stand in the way of achieving the main objectives of economic and social policies. Clearly, in Western Europe and in the European Community in particular there is a general wish to reduce urgently the 11% average unemployment rate. But does this require substantial modification of the European model?

Our thesis here is that in Western Europe today there is a need for some correction of excesses of labor market regulation and social security programs, notably where these stand in the way of a major improvement in the employment situation. This correction needs to be effected in a discriminating way if it is to be both efficient and capable of securing widespread support in public opinion. The fundamentals of the social security system to which Europe is accustomed need not be called into question, at least at the level of ensuring basic health, education, retirement, and income-maintenance benefits. Amendment of labor market and social security policies can fit into a positive model for the Western European political economy, rather than appear as a war of attrition against the social achievements of the postwar era. These amendments could be at the heart of a five to ten year program to return Europe to a high-employment society, overcoming the past decade's experience of a high-unemployment society. Europe's model could not be justified if it did not provide for this.

In the next chapter we set out the arguments in economics and political science that bear on the choice of policy strategy in the labor market and social security areas. The approach is basically to ask the question, How flexible and competitive does the European labor market need to be? What qualifications to the neoclassical paradigm of competitive market conditions are warranted in the labor market and social security domains?

In chapter 3 we review the actual state of a number of labor market and social security policies in Western European countries, the United States, and Japan. The selection of policy instruments is not at all exhaustive, but we look succinctly at some core features of the socioeconomic model and identify where policy corrections seem most clearly to be called for.

The final chapter outlines how these policy reforms could contribute significantly to securing a fundamental improvement in the employment situation, without prejudicing the main qualities of the European socioeconomic model. On the contrary, they would improve it.

2 Theoretical Models for Employment and Social Policies

Here we set out theories governing the desirability of different degrees of flexibility or rigidity in the labor market and show how these fit in with macroeconomic theory. The objective is to understand what kind of market-improving policy reforms may be warranted in Europe, or at least to narrow the chasm of misunderstanding that separates antagonistic viewpoints. For example, on the one hand, those of strong free market, neo-classical convictions give at times the impression of wanting to mount a general offensive against any institutional and policy-based impediments to a highly flexible and automatically clearing labor market. On the other hand, others react in a completely defensive manner to questions about whether institutions and legislation are optimal, as if such questions were the thin end of the wedge that threatened to reverse decades of social progress. This school also tends to claim that macroeconomic policy can largely solve unemployment problems, whereas the neoclassical school denies the possibility that macroeconomic policy can affect durably the level of employment or economic activity. The main purpose in surveying the theoretical literature is to point out that there is more than mere compromise supporting a middle-ground position. The attempt to build a middle-ground social consensus can be based on more positive foundations.

2.1   Competitive Models of Neoclassical Inspiration

Those of neoclassical and monetarist persuasions argue that unemployment tends to converge on a natural rate and that macroeconomic demand policies are capable only of an ephemeral influence on the level of real economic activity and labor demand (Friedman 1968; Minford 1983; Barro 1984). However, it is not only those who take a pessimistic view of the effectiveness of macroeconomic policies who are concerned with the natural rate of unemployment in Europe of the 1980s (Layard et al. 1984). Many economists would tend to the view that macroeconomic demand expansion could on its own deal with some but by no means all of Europe's 11% unemployment rate. This leaves a large amount of unemployment that is not caused by insufficient macroeconomic demand (non-Keynesian unemployment).

The natural rate of unemployment is the rate to which the economy tends because of frictional unemployment as people move from old jobs or schooling to new jobs, increased by further factors that impede the matching of supply and demand in the labor force. The principal factors are usually argued to be rigidity in the wage level and the institutional influences that account for this rigidity. Macroeconomic demand policies attempting to lower unemployment below the natural rate will cause accelerating inflation.

As regards the importance of the wage level as a determinant of employment, it is frequently estimated in econometric work (Layard et al. 1985) that a 1% decrease in the real wage level will lead, after a several year adjustment lag, to about a 1% higher level of employment. This would be at a given level of aggregate demand and so implies significant possiblities for labor-for-capital substitution in the structure of production. Whether the level of demand would be the same is an important but separate question. Many economists would recognize that wage reduction on unchanged macroeconomic policies might weaken demand for a transitional period of a few years. But this depends on how one defines unchanged policies. An unchanged target for the evolution of nominal gross domestic product (GDP) would be one way of avoiding such problems of transitional deflation. This, however, implies blending neo-classical wage policy with Keynesian demand policy, to which we devote more attention later.

Employment protection regulations may be seen as increasing the fixed cost of labor. Such provisions impose direct costs of dismissal through compensation payments as a function of length of service or further indirect costs through delaying or even excluding the possibility of dismissing excess personnel. The perceived cost of these provisions depends on the enterprise's estimate of the probability of the labor force becoming excessive and the cost therefore of excess salaries or compensation payments. These perceived costs may then be analogous to ordinary wage costs, with analogous effects on the propensity to employ.

The generosity of unemployment compensation, both in the level of percentage replacement of prior salary and the period of time and conditions of its availability, is seen as affecting both the supply and the demand side of the labor market. Generous unemployment compensation persuades more people to be choosier over whether to work or what job to accept. It also affects the bargaining position of trade unions, in that a generous unemployment scheme may make unions less fearful of settlements that cost jobs. Several other categories of social security benefits have similar effects on unemployment benefits, notably income-maintenance programs that take over when unemployment benefits end and early retirement and disability pensions, where these are awarded essentially for economic rather than medical reasons.

Minimum wage legislation can reduce employment by excluding the possibility for some potential employment contracts to be made. Some jobs may be available below but not at the minimum wage, and some unemployed persons may be willing to work for less than the minimum wage. More complex minimum wage structures, such as those fixed in some countries for each industry branch, may have more pervasive impacts on preventing a matching of supply and demand in the labor market. Government-regulated changes in the minimum wage may also have a pervasive influence on the evolution of much more of the economy's salary structure, with higher wages sometimes indexed on the minimum wage.

The policy agenda for those of neoclassical persuasion follows accordingly. Trade union power may be reduced, as in the United States, with progressive losses in trade union representation in many industries, the United Kingdom, with legislation to make unions legally liable for damages and to prevent secondary picketing practises, and recently Germany, with withdrawal of unemployment compensation for those laid off because of strikes. Political pressures may be applied directly to achieve lower pay rises, for example, through legislated income policies such as those recently implemented in Belgium, Denmark, and the Netherlands. Employment security may be left unregulated by law, as in the United States, or the severity of legal constraints on dismissals may be reduced, as is discussed in some European countries in chapter 3. The minimum wage may be kept low and declining in real terms, as in the United States, or be reduced in its coverage, as envisaged in the United Kingdom, or in its level, as recently in the Netherlands. Unemployment and other income-maintenance programs may be applied at lower levels of replacement of previous salary or more restrictively in terms of eligibility criteria.

2.2   Efficiency Models of Wage Rigidity and Employment Security

The neoclassical arguments are of undoubted importance, but they are not the whole story. It may be observed empirically that substantial unemployment can persist alongside weak trade unions, little or no employment protection law, and meager social security—as the example of the United States shows. Does this mean that deregulation programs and the rollback of social security need to be redoubled even from this starting point? Or are there other microeconomic justifications, more favorable to various labor market and social policy rigidities, to be entered into the equation?

Economics, sociology, and management science all have contributions to make supporting the second formulation.

In economics, writings in the school of "efficiency wage" theory provide a generic reply that qualifies the neoclassical paradigm, at least in a form so far stated [for general reviews of this literature, see Stiglitz (1984), Akerlof and Yellen (forthcoming), and Katz (1986)]. Efficiency wage theory is concerned with explanations of why firms find it unprofitable to cut wages in the presence of involuntary unemployment. The theory postulates that a firm's production costs may be minimized through paying a wage in excess of that which would clear the labor market (that is, eliminate involuntary unemployment). The basic idea is that higher-than-market-clearing wages will induce higher-than-minimal work effort. More precisely, if the elasticity of work effort with respect to the wage level is unity or more, then the firm will not reduce its production costs when reducing its wages. As a result, there may be involuntary unemployment in a general equilibrium situation in the economy, even in the absence of policy-induced rigidities, such as a minimum wage, or institutional rigidities, such as trade union power.

The literature offers several reasons why this work effort effect should take place. The forerunner of recent contributions is Leibenstein (1976), who coined the term "x-efficiency" to denote the productivity differences observed in individual enterprises and economies that cannot be traced to mainstream economic explanations such as the volume and the technological quality of investment and labor.

Recent contributions advance several reasons for efficiency wages, which, following Katz (1986), may be labeled the shirking model, the labor turnover model, the sociological model, the union threat model, and the dual labor market model.

According to the shirking model, companies combine above-market-clearing wage levels with a freedom to dismiss shirking workers, because then the cost of dismissal to the shirking worker becomes significant. The worker maintains a high work effort to avoid having to turn to lower paid jobs. This argument is more relevant to the United States model of relatively free firing rules than to Europe and Japan, where dismissals are often much more constrained.

According to the labor turnover model, companies paying higher wages obtain a lower rate of turnover. As a result, they incur lower costs in searching for and training new staff and through losing people with valuable experience.

The sociological model describes why people work with more than minimum effort in teamwork with people they come to like or in an organization toward which they develop feelings of loyalty and affection. This is also the case where workers feel they are relatively well treated financially, better, for example, than the minimum going rate for the skill in question in the open market.

The union threat model represents the willingness of firms to pay above-minimum market salaries in order to avoid costs of industrial dispute and/or to prevent unionization of the work force, the latter argument again being more relevant to the United States than to Europe.

The dual labor market model is set out by Bulow and Summers (1985). The primary market exists typically in large enterprises with jobs that entail participation in a complex production process vulnerable to disruption and in which the control of individual work performance may be difficult. The secondary market consists of simpler, relatively menial jobs that can be more easily supervised. In the primary labor market wages tend to be higher, and as a result the prospect of losing such a job is costly to the worker if he or she has to turn to the secondary market for alternative employment. The firm is not interested in reducing the primary job salary to secondary market levels because it would thereby lose its sanction over the productivity of the worker. In this view the existence of a dual labor market is not an indication of market failure or distortion. On the contrary, attempts to prevent the development of a dual market may be both inefficient and harmful to aggregate employment.

Related ideas are found in "implicit contract" literature (Rosen 1985). It is argued that an employment contract often embodies an element of implicit insurance extended by the enterprise to the individual. The purpose of the insurance element is to ensure medium-term stability of income and employment security to the individual, who is less well adapted to face risks of uneven business cycle developments than the enterprise. By contrast, the enterprise normally has an equity capital base and borrowing possibilities that permit it to make such implicit insurance contracts. In principle, the enterprise receives its premium by paying wages of a somewhat lower average level and certainly with less fluctuations than if the individuals were employed on a strictly temporary basis.

Implicit contract theory brings out a further argument in addition to some of the efficiency wage theories of why competitive and profit-maximizing enterprise have reasons to prefer elements of stickiness in employment contracts. It is not only on the trade union side or as a result of public policy in the social security and labor regulation domains that pressures arise for some degree of rigidity in employment conditions. To seek to erode these elements of efficient rigidity by acting on trade union power or social security policy would not be pertinent or efficient.

A number of business school economists and management

scientists in the United States are currently concerned with the "human resource management" policies of industrial enterprises (Walton and Lawrence 1985). Their attention focuses on some features of the United States industrial relations tradition that seems to be poorly adapted to the needs of restoring competitiveness to United States manufacturing, faced in particular with a sharp Japanese challenge. In the numerous comparative studies made of United States and Japanese management methods, the issue of optimal labor turnover frequently arises (Thurow 1985b; Ouchi 1981). The American tradition of free hiring and firing policies and rapid labor turnover is associated with a reluctance to invest sufficiently in staff training, difficulties in ensuring good quality control and staff loyalty, internal rigidities in the organization of jobs, and resistance to technological change. In heavily unionized enterprises there is often a long record of adversarial industrial relations. By contrast, a number of conspicuously successful US enterprises (such as IBM and Hewlett Packard) follow different human resource management policies. They stress the permanence of employment as part of a policy that promotes continuous technical and professional training of staff and constant adaptability to rapidly changing technology in products and production methods.

These characteristics are features of Japanese management methods, especially in large industrial enterprises. There, the larger part of the labor force is composed of "regular" (that is, lifetime) employees, the number of hierarchical grades and job categories is typically rather small, and in-service training is a strong feature. Extensive worker participation also contributes to the objective of harmonious industrial relations and willingness to sustain a rapid pace of technological and productivity advances. Employment security for the majority of employees is nonetheless associated with elements of flexibility, as seen in a relatively flexible bonus pay element and in dual labor market features (a minority of temporary workers with reduced status and advantages).

Critics of the adversarial tradition of US industrial relations, such as Piore and Sabel (1984), draw attention to some exotic practices in unionized manufacturing firms. Their thesis is that external labor market flexibility (that is, free hiring and firing regimes) leads to internal labor market rigidity. By contrast, external security of employment allows employees to be more open to internal flexibility of work organization, introduction of new technologies, etc. According to Piore (1986) the prototype system for unionized blue-collar workers in the United States consists of a complex system of job security rules and job classifications accompanying the free hiring and firing convention. These features of the system interact in ways that make dismissals more costly to the enterprise than is apparent at first sight. In the US unionized sector, dismissals respect seniority rules to the point that, if a highly ranked job is eliminated, the incumbent is transferred to the next job down on the seniority ladder with a bumping of successive employees until the process reaches the last hired person, who is the one laid off.

The disadvantages of free hiring regimes are argued by Piore and Sabel (1984) and Boyer (1985) to be increasing as a result of profound changes in production technologies. This relates to what is sometimes described as the demise of "Taylorism" (monotonous production line assembly work) and the advent of "flexible specialization." The latter results from advances in computer and information technology, permitting great economies in production methods for small job lots of different specifications. In this kind of work environment it becomes much more critical to ensure that the work force attains high standards of technical skills and a readiness to work cooperatively in a constantly changing way.

2.3   Political Models of Neocorporatist Inspiration

In section 2.2 we pointed out microeconomic and microsociological qualifications to the neoclassical paradigm. In the present section we introduce some macroeconomic and macro-sociological ones. Political scientists have in recent years given increased attention to what has been termed "neocorporatism" (Schmitte and Lehmbruch 1979; Lehmbruch and Schmitte 1982). Neocorporatism concerns how the cooperation of inter-est groups, principally trade unions and employers' organiza-tions, may help government and society reach such objectives as high employment and productivity levels and income distri-bution equity. One analyst of neocorporatism (Katzenstein 1983) defines neocorporatism as the

voluntary cooperative regulation of conflicts over economic and social issues through highly structured and interpenetrated sets of political relationships by business, the unions, and the state, aug-mented at times by political parties . . . .

"Strong" corporatist structures have a pervasive ideology of social partnership shared by the leaders of business and the unions, rely on the cooperative efforts of relatively centralized institutions represent-ing business, unions, and the state in key economic and social policies, and lack in worker militancy. "Weak" corporatist structures lack an ideology of social partnership, rely on conflictual efforts of relatively decentralized institutions . . . and display considerable worker mili-tancy. (pp. 116–117)

A motivation for the study of neocorporatism comes from the need to explain the extremely high standards of economic welfare achieved in a number of small industrialized countries in Europe, especially in Scandinavia, Switzerland, and Austria. Germany and Japan also have achieved high levels of efficiency and income distribution equity. All these countries are consid-ered to be rather corporatist. By contrast, the United States, while achieving high levels of macroeconomic productivity, has a competitive market system and ethos that has not ensured a comparable level of economic equity. The United States is doubtless the least neocorporatist of the Western industrialized countries.

The hypothesis is that a well-functioning system of neocorporatism may bring considerable benefits through cooperation between labor and employers and, on a tripartite basis with government, over such issues as the coherence of income bargaining with macroeconomic policy, the achievement of harmony rather than conflict in industrial relations, and the amenability of labor to the dissemination of technical progress in the workplace.

Neocorporatism presents a challenge to the neoclassical paradigm because it involves a positive role for interest groups, such as trade unions, that normally place a high value on social policies that give income distribution equity and job security. The instruments of equity and security are largely those of social security finance, income bargaining, and employment protection rules. But these instruments are also central to the incentive structure affecting work, employment and investment and to the regulatory environment conditioning employment. As related before, neoclassical arguments may be used to favor increased financial incentives and deregulation of the labor market in order to achieve the efficiency and employment goals of society. The neocorporatist argument counters this by pointing out the economic losses that may result from conflicting industrial relations and incompatibilities between, for example, high pay settlements and macroeconomic policy targets. The complete evaluation of a given microeconomic policy move, for example, to improve work incentives through diminishing unemployment benefits, has to take into account the possible impact on the cooperativeness of the social partners in their various activities.

How can one assess this "neocorporatist cost" against the "neoclassical benefit" of a given microeconomic policy change? The question may be put more broadly: When will an action sharpening microeconomic work incentives but curtailing income or employment security induce a net positive impact on the productivity of the economy? When may the net effect even be negative? Answers may be sought in two types of evidence, one institutional and the other econometric.

Some political scientists have attempted to measure objective criteria making for strong corporatism and to rank industrialized countries accordingly. Criteria that favor corporatism are considered to be (1) the extent of trade union membership, the unity or cohesiveness of leadership of the trade unions ensured by its peak organizations, and the ability of the peak organizations to deliver shop floor adherence to centrally negotiated deals; (2) similar qualities of membership, unity, and leadership among employers' organizations; (3) the importance of work councils or other cooperative bodies bringing workers and management together in the enterprise; and (4) the importance of the range of policy issues over which effective consultations are carried out on a tripartite basis among government, labor, and employers.

One ranking of the strength of corporatism, based on a weighting of indicators representing the foregoing criteria, has been suggested by Crouch (1984) and adapted by Bruno and Sachs (1985):

1. Austria
2. Germany
3. The Netherlands
4. Norway
5. Sweden
6. Denmark
7. Switzerland
8. Finland
9. Japan
10. Belgium
11. Italy
12. France
13. United Kingdom
14. United States

The list is headed by the small northern European countries and Germany. Japan follows, receiving high points for concertation of labor and employers at the enterprise level but scoring less high on tripartism on public policy issues. Italy and France have some corporatist traditions and institutions, but in both cases the ideological splits and the militancy of trade unions and their limited representation bring down the corporatist score. The United Kingdom score is brought down by the highly fragmented and competitive craft structure of the trade union movement, coupled with highly conflictual tendencies in industrial relations. Finally, the United States ranks lowest because of low membership and weak central leadership roles of labor and employers' organizations. Lobbying in Washington sees much activity by multifarious interest groups, but negotiation over matters of economic or social policy between government and unified representatives of labor and employers is largely absent from the system.

This rough ordering is an indication of the capacity of corporatist structures to deliver benefits or threaten costs to the government as they execute policies that may be more or less welcome to the major interest groups. In the hypothesis of policies of neoclassical inspiration designed to sharpen competition in the labor market, the practical question is whether such initiatives risk eroding the cooperativeness of labor in the enterprise or at the level of national policy making or, conversely, whether policy initiatives offering greater social security may win more effective cooperation on other issues of policy.

For the least corporatist countries, such as the United States, the inference is that policy choices over, for example, social security or labor law, may be taken more narrowly on the direct merits of the given measure. Wider repercussions of such measures are least likely to be important, compared to other more corporatist countries. Similarly, in the United Kingdom the Conservative government of the 1980s felt that there was little to lose from actions to curtail union powers, given the frequent failure of trade unions to deliver their part of cooperative policy pacts in earlier administrations. As corporatist strength increases, that is, as one moves up in the list, the importance of calculating the impact of policy initiatives on the cooperativeness of the social partners increases.

An interesting attempt has been made recently by Weisskopf (1985) to test econometrically whether increasing social security in the main industrialized countries has been associated in the last fifteen years with an improved or worsened productivity performance. According to the hypothesis, in relatively strong corporatist countries increased social security would encourage cooperative behavior on the part of labor and thus help to improve productivity (in a "class-harmony" model). In weakly corporatist countries such policies would merely diminish microeconomic incentives to work effort and so result in weaker productivity growth (in a "class-conflict" model). Such econometric tests should no doubt be considered rather heroic on the grounds that roughly aggregated indicators of policy variables, with the aid of a simplified model of the economy, are taken to explain macroeconomic behavior. With this reserve it is to be noted that Weisskopf finds some support for the hypothesis that in the long run the productivity impact of enhanced social security (defined as social transfer payments to people of working age) differed according to the corporatist qualities of the economy. Highly corporatist countries (Sweden, Germany, and Japan) showed some positive association of productivity advance and increased social security. Weakly corporatist countries (the United States, the United Kingdom, Italy) showed some negative impact on productivity trends of increased social security. The evidence is not so clear-cut because the findings differ in some cases according to whether short- or long-run associations are studied. Nevertheless, indications are given of different behavioral reactions of the economy to changes in social security systems, and these lend some support for the possibility of contrary class-conflict versus class-harmony reactions, depending on the quality of corporatist organization of society.

Bruno and Sachs (1985) also found evidence, in a study of seventeen industrialized countries during the first seven oil-shock years (1973 to 1980), that a high ranking in corporatism is associated with a low rise in the "misery index" (the sum of the unemployment and inflation rates). Such countries included Austria, the Netherlands, Germany, Norway, Denmark, and Switzerland. Conversely, countries with a low corporatism index suffered higher adjustment costs in this period; these countries include Italy, the United Kingdom, and France.

A recent study by Bean et al. (1986) has carried this line of investigation further. They have examined econometrically, with data covering 1953 to 1983, the lags with which the labor market and its wage mechanisms in particular react to situations in which unemployment has been created by shocks, such as rises in taxes or import prices. Bean et al. find that there is a significantly more rapid adjustment in corporatist countries. Wages in the more corporatist countries respond more quickly to unemployment and even more strongly to changes in taxes and import prices. Wages thus rise less fast as unemployment rises or when tax or import price increases threaten the profit margins of enterprises. The mean lag found with this variety of adjustment processes was around three years in the least corporatist countries (Italy, the United Kingdom, the United States) and under a year for the most corporatist European countries and Japan.

Observations for the early 1980s may have seen some weakening of the inverse relationship between corporatism and the evolution of the misery index. The uncorporatist United States has improved its relative performance, whereas some of the most corporatist European countries have encountered increasing problems (relatively high inflation in Sweden, relatively high unemployment in Germany and the Netherlands). Some commentators see signs of a demise of neocorporatism and ascendency of the neoclassical competitive model. However, such conclusions may be premature or exaggerated. Cyclical factors should not be allowed to distort evidence of these long-run societal characteristics. For example, it would be advisable to await a return of the United States economy to a sustainable position in its external accounts and public finances before drawing conclusions from current experience.

Some analysts from the Scandinavian school, although basically sympathetic to cooperative and solidaristic models of political economy, nonetheless draw attention to possible weaknesses of this system. In particular, Calmfors (1985a, b), in an analysis of the European countries representing the corporatist traditions, draws attention to the situation in which centralized wage bargaining is combined with macroeconomic policies that are more or less accommodating to inflation (for example, Sweden and Finland, where macroeconomic policies have been relatively accommodating, compared to Germany, where policy has been nonaccommodating). The wage behavior of centralized trade unions is interpreted as differing crucially according to whether government policies are expected to be accommodating or not. Where macroeconomic policies are, in the light of experience, expected to be accommodating, trade union wage claims are less moderate rather than more so.

2.4 Some Eclectic Contributions from Mainstream Macroeconomics

Fortunately, modern macroeconomic theory does not let matters rest with these contradictory strands of thinking—with the neoclassical model advocating greater flexibility in labor markets and the efficiency wage and neocorporatist models resisting such suggestions in some degree.

Mainstream macroeconomic theory and empirical analysis encourage a more eclectic view of how the economy works and how unemployment is determined in particular. The main insights of the neoclassical and neo-Keynesian schools are increasingly integrated in theory and empirical analysis. Extreme and monolithic theories do not commend majority support among economists, be they Keynesian, neoclassical, or rational-expectations monetarist. Contributions in the sense of a modern synthesis include some leading texts on macroeconomic theory: Dornbusch and Fischer (1981), Hall and Taylor (1985), and Malinvaud et al. (1981–1982). Drèze (1986) offers a short theoretical explanation of how the different strands of unemployment theory may be integrated. These indeas are also becoming reflected in mainstream macroeconometric models of industrial countries, which were reviewed in a recent Brookings research project (Bryant et al., forthcoming). This project compared a dozen multicountry world models. Special-purpose empirical investigations of unemployment trends in the industrialized countries have recently been brought together in a volume edited by Bean et al. (1986), with a valuable cross-country study by the editors, and a more aggregated study for the European Community and the United States by Bruno (1986).

The basic message emerging from all these contributions is that both macroeconomic demand and the level of real labor costs matter for the level of employment.

Macroeconomic demand policies, budgetary and monetary, may be less of a universal medicine for unemployment problems than supposed in the 1960s—the years of the postwar Keynesian consensus. But the more adequate representation, as in the models reviewed by Bryant et al., of monetary and neoclassical supply-side factors has far from totally reduced macroeconomic policy to the state of impotence postulated by some theorists. Simulations for the European Community economy, set out in appendix B, illustrate this. These simulation results are very much in the middle of those reviewed by Bryant et al. The simulations for the European Community economy show a fiscal policy expansions (an expansion in government investment with money supply held unchanged) as having a first-year multiplier impact on gross domestic product (GDP) of about 1 during the first three years (that is, a 1% of GDP increase in public investment leads to an increase of 1% in GDP itself). This impact on GDP reaches a peak multiplier of 1.2 in the second year, before gradually declining over the third to sixth years as interest rate increases have a compensating, contractionary influence.

Within the same model of the European economy, presented in appendix B, or in the simplified reduced-form models of Bean et al. (1986) and Bruno (1986), the impact of changes in real wages and profitability are seen to have a significant impact on employment. In the simulations reported in appendix B, a real wage change of 1% affects the level of employment only slightly in the first instance (in the first to third years) but builds up in the medium-term quite strongly. A 1% increase in the employment level is achieved by year 5, as a result of a 1% real wage reduction. This figure is broadly consistent with the findings of Layard et al. (1985) already reported.

A separate question from the effects of labor costs on employment is how the changes in labor costs may be engineered. At this point the macroeconometric models generally need to be complemented by more details of an institutional nature. The alternative approaches of both neoclassical and neocorporatist inspiration can be considered. In the first case, sharper incentives in the labor market would be the instrument. In this context social security provisions and employment protection regulations are important; these policies are discussed in chapter 3. In the second case, politically organized incomes policies would be the instrument. Different blends of the two approaches are also possible. Both can properly find their place in the framework of mainstream macroeconomic theory.

Two contributions, those of Malinvaud (1981–1982) and Meade (1982), deserve special mention. Both are explicitly addressed to the integration of neoclassical and neo-Keynesian theories of unemployment.

Malinvaud is to be credited with the major initiative of reinscribing a classical theory of unemployment into a general macroeconomic theory of a basically Keynesian structure. Malinvaud analyzes unemployment as being of two types: "classical," resulting from excess real wages, and "Keynesian," resulting from insufficient macroeconomic demand, with possibilities for the economy to switch between varying mixes of unemployment of these two types. The underlying theoretical specification is beginning to be reflected in applied econometric models, for example in the model of the European Community economy summarized in appendix B [see also Dramais (1986)].

A further contribution in the sense of a Keynesian and classical synthesis is offered by Meade (1982) and Vines et al. (1983). Meade calls his approach New-Keynesian. He advocates a positive demand management policy, targeted on keeping the evolution of nominal demand (alternatively called money demand, or nominal gross domestic product) on a path set and announced by the government for a medium-term period ahead. Nominal demand allows for a real and an inflation component, with a split between the two to be determined by wage trends and other microeconomic policies affecting productivity. Although this split is elastic, the overall target for nominal demand sets a nonaccommodating outer limit for inflation. The level of employment, in Meade's conception, is then determined by the wage level, given the targeted level of nominal demand. Meade's wage policy is therefore quite classical in inspiration, whereas his demand policy is Keynesian. Policy simulations in this spirit have been set out for the European economy in the Cooperative Growth Strategy advocated by the Commission of the European Communities in its recent annual economic reports (1985, 1986a).

Meade proposes a particular arbitration system for settling wages at levels that ensure high employment. His precise ideas relate especially to the United Kingdom, but the broad idea is of wider relevance. Other economists offer alternative wage policies that fit into the same family of theoretical ideas, for example, Weitzman (1984), who favors a profit-linked pay element to ensure sufficient overall real wage flexibility to facilitate maintenance of a high-employment level.

Some recent analysts of the European unemployment problem have focused on what they call the "hysteresis" hypothesis (Sachs 1985; Blanchard and Summers 1986a, b). This is a further eclectic theory of unemployment, drawing on both Keynesian and classical ideas. The hypothesis is that the unemployment level has strong inertial features, which naturally tend to a maintenance of high or low unemployment levels, irrespective of the particular causal path that led to a given level. The current high level of European unemployment is analyzed by economists of neoclassical persuasion as being due to a high "natural" rate caused by institutional-policy-induced rigidities in the wage system. The alternative hysteresis view is that there may be no fixed "natural" rate and that a burst of rapid growth may overcome what looks like a high natural or classical rate of unemployment. For example, the prewar period of high unemployment was ended by the military buildup in the Second World War.

In conclusion, it is apparent that the foregoing elements of theory are not in all cases integrated into a consistent whole. Microeconomic theory still needs to properly integrate different arguments favoring elements both of flexibility and rigidity in the labor market. There are contributions, however, in which modified Keynesian macroeconomic policies and neoclassically inspired wage policies are fitted together coherently. Policy advisers have to make their own implicit synthesis of economic theory. The next chapters review certain domains of policy and offer some conclusions for their evolution in Europe in this spirit.

3

Core Features of the Socioeconomic Model in Practice

3.1   Pay Systems

The pay systems of Western Europe are quite heterogeneous with respect to such features as the level of centralization of bargaining, the degree of intervention of governments with incomes policies, the degree of wage-price indexation, and the role of minimum wage legislation. These systems have been analyzed in great detail by Flanagan et al. (1983), in their study on incomes policies in Western Europe, and more recently and briefly by Bruno and Sachs (1985). Rather than attempting to cover this ground again, here we focus on some aspects that have particular bearing on Europe's unemployment problem, especially where there are important contrasts to be made with the pay determination systems of the United States and Japan. These topics are, first, the desirable degree of flexibility of wages as a function of different economic conditions and, second, the role of minimum wage rules in dampening horizontal wage flexibility (by region, skill, company size, etc.). The general issue is the balance to be struck in the labor market between price and quantity adjustments. Where prices are fixed, quantities bear the burden of adjustment in response to changing supply and demand conditions. If prices are flexible, changes in quantity will be minimal. In the European labor market the price of labor has tended to be particularly rigid, and the quantity of labor has had to adjust to an alarming degree, as evidenced by the rise in unemployment from $2\frac{1}{2}$% in 1973 to 11% in 1986 and the decline of the labor force participation. For men aged 16 to 64 the decline in the participation rate from 1973 to 1983 was particularly sharp, from 89% to 82%.

As regards the flexibility of pay over time, a model case is seen in Japan. The notable feature of Japanese pay determination is the relatively important role of bonus payments, usually paid twice a year, complementing the weekly or monthly base wage. In recent years bonus payments in Japan have constituted on average about 25% of a worker's pay. Bonus payments are more variable than base wages. Weitzman (1985) has calculated that at an aggregate level they display three times as much variability as base wages and even more so at an individual industry level. Some companies, such as Toyota, try to keep the bonus payment at a stable number of months pay. Other companies, such as those in the machine tools or shipbuilding industries, have seen their bonus payments vary between zero and ten months' pay. The majority of firms are in an intermediate position between these two extremes. The degree of linkages of bonus payments to profits is, in view of these divergent practices, variable. Regression analysis by Weitzman (1985) suggests that on average a 10% variation in profits leads to a 1.4% variation in the level of the bonus.

This element of flexibility in bonus payment appears in econometric studies of the response of wages to price and supply shocks. A representative set of estimates are those calculated by Coe (1985), summarized in table 3.1. These estimates show Japan's pay system to have performed in the period since the 1973 oil shock in a manner favorable to the maintenance of the level of employment. This study shows that it has taken only a 0.28% increase in Japanese unemployment to result in the extinction of an upward shock to the price level of 1%. By comparison, the same estimates came out with around five to ten times as high values in Europe and only a little less in the

Table 3.1
Measures of short- and long-run real wage rigidity

Country	Short-run real wage rigidity[a]	Long-run real wage rigidity[a]
United States	0.67	3.06
Japan	0.28	0.28
France	1.52	3.03
Germany	1.76	3.52
Italy	1.48	1.48
United Kingdom	1.94	5.82
The Netherlands	1.07	2.14
Austria	0.83	1.67
European average[b]	1.4	2.9

Source: Coe (1985).
a. A value of unity implies that a 1% increase in the unemployment rate would be required to offset a real shock that would otherwise result in a 1% increase in the price level. Higher values thus imply a higher increase in unemployment to be required, and lower values a lower increase in unemployment.
b. Unweighted average of the countries shown.

United States. These findings are in keeping with what the flexibility of the bonus system in Japan would lead one to expect. Automatically and before large labor market disequilibria have to develop, the wage levels adjust to the profit-reducing and inflationary impact of shocks, such as the oil price increases of 1973 to 1982. In Europe it is apparent that a painfully large increase in unemployment has to develop before a significant wage adjustment takes place.

The main features of pay determination in the United States are its extreme decentralization under 195,000 different bargaining agreements, which even so cover only 25% of the labor force, and the weak influence of the minimum wage. The federally legislated minimum wage in 1986 was $3.35 an hour and has been unchanged since 1981. It is now under one-third the average wage level (Bureau of Labor Statistics, 1986). Moreover, the average real wage level has also remained remarkably constant in the course of the last four years of business upswing.

By comparison, wage bargaining is in most European countries much more centralized and often subject to more constraining minimum wage laws or conventions. Minimum wages in Europe are set in several different ways. Five countries have statutory national minimum wages (France, Luxembourg, the Netherlands, Portugal, and Spain). In two countries (Belgium and Greece) a national minimum wage is set by collective bargaining at the national level and given support by law for its enforcement. In three countries (Denmark, Germany, and Italy) minimum pay rates are set at the industry level by collective bargaining and have the force of law. In Belgium, too, industry-level minima are set for many branches of the economy above the national minimum. In two countries (the United Kingdom and Ireland) industry-level minima are set for industries in which union representation is often weak. In France in 1985 the minimum wage was as high as 70% of the average wage in manufacturing; in Belgium and the Netherlands it was even higher, about 75%. The level of minima set in Germany and Italy may be no less constraining in relation to average wage levels than the French and Benelux examples just quoted (this is a topic deserving further study).

European minimum wage laws do usually have one desirable degree of flexibility: prescribing lower levels of minimum pay for young workers (European Industrial Relations Review, 1986). Typically the minimum wage for given ages is expressed as a percentage of the adult minimum. For example at 18 years old the percentage is 77.5% in Belgium, 45% in the Netherlands, but already 95% in Portugal, and 100% in France, Greece, and Spain. In the United States the idea of a subminimum wage for youths has been debated but not decided on.

The Japanese minimum wage system has some interesting features ("Minimum Wage in Japan," 1985). It is set separately at the level of the forty-seven prefectures by the local authorities after tripartite consultation with trade unions and employer organizations. Prefectures are placed in one of four ranks, with different minimum wage levels. In 1985 the range of minimum wages was lowest at ¥395 per hour in relatively backward regions, ¥455 per hour in Kyoto, and highest at ¥477 per hour in Tokyo. Thus the extreme regional spread of minimum wages was some 25%. At early 1987 exchange rates (¥150 to the dollar), the minimum wage ranges between $2.64 and $3.19 per hour, somewhat below the US minimum wage of $3.35 per hour but much less than some European minimum wages (that of Belgium in 1985 was $4.90 per hour, at the current exchange of Fr38 to the dollar). The ratio between the Japanese minimum wage and average wages (1 to 3−3.5) is similar to that of the United States (1 to 3.3). In reality the Japanese minimum wage may be less constraining, as there is a higher uniformity of educational standards in Japan compared with the United States, which has a substantial minority of functionally illiterate persons in its labor force. Europe's degree of educational homogeneity is somewhere between that of Japan and the United States, and possibly closer to Japan.

The effects of minimum wage laws on wage structures, especially those fixed at the level of each industry, should be revealed in statistics on wage differentials by size of enterprise, with small firms tending to pay lower wages. It turns out that in the United States small firms' wages (firms with 10 to 99 employees) are much lower relative to those of large firms (with over 500 employees) than in Europe and Japan. Data published by the OECD (1985b) show the ratio of small to large firm wages to be 57% in the United States, 77% in Japan, 78% in Belgium, 83% in France, 85% in Italy, 90% in Germany, and 93% in Denmark.

The centralization of wage bargaining, the extent of union

power, and the minimum wage would all influence the extent of interindustry wage differentials. Data on the coefficient of variation in industry wage levels, also provided by the OECD (1985b), confirm other indicators showing the United States to be twice as flexible in this respect as the typical European country. The coefficient of variation of industry branch wage levels (standard deviation as percentage of the mean) in the early 1980s was 23% in the United States and ranged from 8% to 11% in France, Germany, Italy, Sweden, the Netherlands, and Denmark. The United Kingdom (15%) and Spain (17%) were in intermediate positions. Of particular interest is the position of Japan, with a coefficient of 26%—an even wider interindustry pay differential than in the United States. This confirms the picture of Japan as an economy combining some notable features of pay flexibility both in evolution and differentials with other features of stability, such as employment security.

It is not easy to make operational proposals for a pay system that can be broadly applied to a region as diverse in its wage-setting behavior as Western Europe. However, the region does have a largely common employment problem and widespread tendencies toward rigidity of real wage levels in the face of labor market disequilibria. Reforms in the area of the mechanisms discussed could, however, be envisaged for many countries: to introduce a profit-based element in the pay package and to render the minimum wage less of a constraint on employment creation. Such reforms should aim to make the European pay systems more competitive and adaptable to changing economic conditions. More precisely, reforms might be envisaged along the following four lines.

1. In all countries with centralized or decentralized modes of pay setting, a distinction between base pay and bonus pay could be introduced. The United Kingdom government in 1986 launched for discussion with the social partners the idea of fiscal incentives to convert, for example, 20% of pay into a profit-

linked bonus. In the United States there is currently some autonomous tendency in this direction in collective bargaining. Bonus pay could have two main forms: a profit-related cash element or a share-participation equity element. The profit-related element would be particularly appropriate where the enterprise is concerned with being able to ride through changing demand and market conditions without having to be unduly cautious in taking on extra employees. The key point in Weitzman's (1984) proposal for profit-linked bonus schemes concerns the likely marginal cost that extra employees would cause at some point in the future when demand conditions might weaken. If the total wage bill had a profit-related element, then the extra cost of marginal employees could be relatively easily absorbed by a degree of flexibility in the total wage bill.

2. A share-participation equity element would be particularly appropriate where a company is quite profitable and wishes to strengthen its capital base while expanding its investment and employment. This is relevant to the present condition of the European economy, which would need a prolonged investment boom in the years ahead in order to absorb into jobs a large number of its present unemployed.

3. Minimum pay systems should be reconsidered with a view to facilitating the employment of those currently excluded from the labor market. In such reforms the idea of a social minimum pay level, intended to avoid economic exploitation of marginal and weak members of society, should be retained. However, the level should not be so high as to deter the creation and expansion of new enterprises with more competitive cost structures drawing on the large pool of unemployed persons. Outsiders in the labor market should not be deprived of the chance to enter the market, which would be subject to policies respecting social minimum pay levels. A national minimum wage should therefore be retained with a suitably low level and possibly with variations allowed for youths and for depressed regions, with

the elimination of monopoly powers for collective bargaining to set mandatory and legally enforceable minimum wages by industry.

4. To strengthen the consensus over the fairness of these degrees of pay flexibility, governments should seek understanding concerning the interaction between pay flexibility and macroeconomic policy. A legitimate concern is that flexibility over pay, notably on the down side, may create negative macroeconomic demand effects, at least in the short run, and dampen or even annul the employment expansion effects of the pay policy. To ease this concern, governments should publish and pursue clear medium-term targets for the evolution of nominal macroeconomic demand (Meade 1982; Vines et al. 1983). In the event that pay policies or other conditions generate an unexpected weakness of nominal demand, this would be regarded as presumptive evidence in favor of more expansionary monetary or fiscal policies. Targets for nominal demand expansion also imply, however, not accommodating inflation beyond certain limits and so can counter the problem alluded to earlier (section 2.3) that accommodating demand policies may induce inflationary wage settlements.

3.2   Hiring and Firing Regulations

Hiring and firing rules lie at the heart of policies of regulation or nonregulation of the labor market. The following types of regulation are involved: rules of recruitment, for example, privileging disadvantaged minorities; rules for individual dismissals; rules for collective redundancies and layoffs; and rules for temporary, part-time, and fixed-term employment.

Liberal employment protection rules would be expected to result in higher cyclical swings in layoffs, dismissals, and recruitment, compared to regimes with greater rigidities imposing costs or delays on short-term changes in the labor force. This is clearly the case in the United States, where employment fluctuations are more pronounced than in Europe or Japan, whose labor markets are much more regulated.

Onerous employment protection rules may be expected to dampen the trend of growth of employment by adding a semi-fixed element to the cost of labor and by encouraging capital-for-labor substitution in the production process. This appears to be the case in Europe, compared notably with the United States, although other factors of course contribute to the evolution of relative factor prices (Mortensen 1984).

There are other arguments concerning the effects of employment protection law on the quality and productivity of labor. It is argued by Piore and Sabel (1984) and by others that a free hiring and firing regime is associated with a lesser propensity of the enterprise to invest in in-house training because of a higher chance of losing this investment and a lesser propensity of workers to cooperate in efficient teamwork. These arguments seem to have a certain validity, but they are of variable importance depending on the type of industry or enterprise. What may be important for a technologically advanced production process may not be important for simpler systems and many service activities, such as shops and restaurants. There is also a counterargument that a shirking worker can have an adverse productivity effect on other workers; the rules and regulations cannot effectively sanction this.

The differences between the models of the United States on the one hand and the models of Europe and Japan on the other are fundamental [details and sources are given in Emerson (1987)]. In the United States, generally there is no federal or state law regulating these issues. The law intervenes only to enforce private contracts. Traditionally, employment can be terminated at will with little or no notice on the initiative of either side. The courts are now tending to place more constraints on the at-will doctrine in cases of disputed individual dismissals. The absence of regulations does not therefore mean an absence of juridical constraints. However, the legal system appears to be getting into increasing difficulty with the escalating growth and cost of litigation in this area, which is due to the absence of general legislation. As for collective redundancies, only 15% of collective bargains contain employment protection clauses. There is also now some tendency toward favoring greater employer security in the personnel policies of large corporations.

Europe and Japan have more in common. In both regions there is a complex set of legal and customary provisions ensuring a great preference for permanent employment and security of tenure. However, the Japanese system retains a more important duality than is generally the case in Europe. In the large Japanese enterprises a minority of positions (around 7%) do not benefit from the regular permanent employment regime, and small Japanese enterprises are able to adjust rather freely the size of their labor force because they typically employ a larger fraction of temporary workers. It is worth noting how this dual system came about. During the Korean War boom many Japanese firms were worried about expanding employment with permanent jobs for what might prove only ephemeral demand. To ease this problem, the Japanese allowed deviations from the permanent job standard, thus permitting a margin of insecure employment.

In Europe there is a considerable range of severity in employment protection regulations. All the large countries, however (France, Germany, Italy, Spain, the United Kingdom), and most of the smaller countries have comprehensive legislation on the statutes, much of which was introduced in the early 1970s. As Blanchard et al. (1985) have pointed out, the perceived cost of given restrictions on dismissals must have increased substantially in the following years, as a long period of recession or low growth set in, and the probability of having excess workers in the average firm increased. In most European countries the legal costs or difficulty of dismissals were therefore increasing just at the time when these probabilities began to rise. So the effective burden of regulation doubly increased.

These important differences in employment protection law should show up in indicators of turnover in the labor market. This is indeed the case. In the United States the percentage of jobs held for under two years is twice as great as in Europe and Japan. Similarly, the annual average turnover of the labor force in the enterprise is twice as great in the United States.

Concern over excessively onerous employment protection laws in many European countries may be founded on several facts: Employment growth has been weak; capital-deepening and labor-saving trends have been evident; employment security has not gone together with wage flexibility (as in Japan); and employment protection laws are of general application and, apart from exonerations for small enterprises, make little allowance for different types of enterprise or employee.

The typical set of employment protection laws runs as follows. As regards individual dismissals, a notice period that depends on length of service is required, criteria for "fair" dismissal are stipulated, amounts of minimum financial compensation are laid down, and procedures for appeal to labor courts in the event of alleged unfair dismissal are established. In some countries the system of judicial appeal is considered to be particularly onerous for the employer because of the length of delay before proceedings are held (Germany) or the probability of outcomes favoring the employer (Italy, Spain, Portugal). By comparison, the British tribunal system appears to be rather evenhanded with respect to the employer and the employee. In about half of the European countries the approval of the work council or trade union or government employment office also has to be obtained, notably in Germany, France (until 1986), the Netherlands, Italy, Spain, and Portugal.

As regards collective redundancies, analogous procedures are generally required. Among European countries only Denmark and Finland leave the terms of redundancies essentially to private contract in collective bargaining and, as in the United States, abstain from statutory regulation.

Regulations governing temporary and fixed-term employment contracts generally support the rules for dismissals and redundancies; otherwise these forms of employment contract would in some degree substitute for permanent contracts governed by restrictive rules. Agencies supplying temporary workers are usually subject to licensing controls in Europe and in Japan, unlike the United States, where there are no such controls. In Sweden and Italy private agencies are even prohibited. Temporary workers are typically restricted to certain types of jobs (seasonal, replacement of absent permanent staff, certain skills, and limited periods of time). Restrictions of maximum duration (usually six months to three years) and limiting criteria for job types also apply to direct employment on fixed-term contracts. When fixed-term contracts are renewed beyond certain limits, the law regards the employee as if serving under permanent contract.

Layoffs, that is, the putting of employees onto reduced times of work without termination of the employment contract, are possible in all industrialized countries. The systems in the United States and Italy prefer total layoffs, whereas most European countries and Japan favor short-time working.

Other regulations constraining recruitment are less widespread. Only the United States has had something approaching a quota system favoring the employment of racial minorities and women in companies receiving federal contracts. The administration sought in 1986 to make these rules voluntary. However, Supreme Court judgments contest this move. European countries mostly apply mandatory quotas favoring the employment of handicapped workers, often of about 6% of employment. Some countries have relatively flexible systems, applying taxes and subsidies for under- and overachievement of the quotas (such as Germany and France). Italy mandates an extraordinarily high 15% quota for handicapped workers, but the result is only 4%.

Italy also has a unique employment regulation: Employment

agencies are empowered to prescribe whom an employer can take on according to an administrative rank ordering of applicants. This system has been attenuated with various exonerations, for example, for certain skills. It now applies to only 50% of an enterprise's recruitment needs. However, the whole system does appear to be exceedingly onerous administratively.

Surveys have recently been carried out in Europe by the Commission of the European Communities (1986b) and the International Employers' Organisation (1985) to obtain qualitative information on the employment impact of this body of regulations. The commission's survey covered the opinions of 50,000 individual enterprises, and the IEO's survey covered the opinions of the head offices of the national employer's organization in each country. Broadly, these two surveys are considerably concordant in their results. They suggest that among the larger countries the regulations are perceived to be very serious in Germany, Italy, and Spain, rather serious in France, but much less serious in the United Kingdom. Among the smaller countries the regulations are perceived to be particularly serious in Belgium, the Netherlands, Sweden, and Portugal; Norway and Austria are in an intermediate category, and Denmark and Finland are judged to have the lightest regulations. The results of the surveys are given in more detail elsewhere (Commission of the European Communities, 1986b).

In considering possible policy reforms for Europe, the most radical option theoretically would be to move from heavy regulation, as at present, to total deregulation, as in the United States. This option is not recommended on three grounds. First, employment protection laws have a complex of effects on the labor market, some positive and some negative. The deregulation option would in this situation be too blunt an approach. Second and illustrating this point, the United States model is itself being questioned. The legal system for litigation over individual dismissals is in considerable disarray, and an increasing number of large enterprises are seeing merit in offering employees greater security of employment. However, these qualifications to the United States model should not be exaggerated, nor should this country's remarkable job creation record be forgotten. Third, however, the Japanese model shows that employment protection law can be reconciled with a good employment record.

The Japanese model also draws attention to the importance of other conditions, notably pay flexibility, discussed earlier, which may be required to reconcile high employment protection with a high employment level in the economy. Greater pay flexibility may be recommended for Europe, but this cannot be easily achieved, certainly not by simple legislation. Therefore European countries need to be extremely careful in extending regulatory constraints on their labor markets.

Given the present European unemployment problem, employment protection laws should be reviewed along the following five lines:

1. General framework regulations should be retained governing individual dismissals and collective redundancies. These provisions should indicate minimum notice periods and amounts of compensation relating to length of service, but several countries should consider revising these variables downward.

2. For individual dismissals the law should set out criteria of what constitutes "fair" dismissal. Unfair dismissal should receive higher compensation or reinstatement. Labor tribunals should provide means of judicial appeal and decision. These tribunals should work expeditiously and represent a fair balance of interest between the employer and employee, which is not at present the case in several countries.

3. For collective dismissals the procedure should include, with reasonable notice periods, consultation with work council or trade union representatives and information from the government employment office. Maximum efforts should be made, and explained, to find alternatives to dismissals, for example, voluntary retirement, short-term work, and transfers between

plants of the same enterprise. However, the decision should remain that of the enterprise, not requiring approval of employees' representatives or authorization of the government; this also would imply changes in several countries.

4. Possibilities for small and medium enterprises to take on new employees with less onerous regulatory constraints should be enlarged.

5. Possibilities for temporary, part-time, and fixed-term contract employment should be adapted to facilitate increased employment opportunities for marginal members of the labor force, especially youths, part-time second-income earners in the family, and older people near or around the normal retirement age. The more liberal use of fixed-term employment contracts for longer periods (eighteen months to three years) may be a particularly useful technique for reducing the burden of employment protection law for new employees while leaving the acquired rights of existing permanent staff unaffected.

3.3   Income Maintenance for Those of Working Age

There are enormous differences between European income-maintenance policies and those in the United States. Taking averages of the states of the two regions, there are perhaps as large spreads between the most generous and parsimonious states of the United States as there are among the nations of Western Europe. The size of public expenditures on income maintenance, broadly defined, is on average twice as great in Europe. Correspondingly, the degree of income equalization achieved by the tax and transfer system or the reduction in the number of people living in poverty as a result of public policies is also much greater in Europe, around two to three times in relative magnitude. These ratios are wider still for people of working age (as table 3.10 in a later section shows).

It is also the case that the employment ratio among people of working age has risen substantially in the United States, whereas it has been declining in Europe. Certainly these labor market trends reflect other influences, such as movements of the business cycle, and other labor market factors already discussed, such as pay and employment regulations. However, there is also reason to believe that income-maintenance systems are important influences as well. Thus differences of choice over what Okun (1975) called the "great trade-off," that between equality and efficiency, stand out immediately in the most summary of comparisons between the United States and Europe.

Unemployment Compensation

All countries have unemployment compensation systems. The criteria of eligibility and length and level of benefits are a complex mass of details (see table A.1 for the main features). Broadly, benefits in the United States are relatively low in percentage of previous pay (50% compared to 60–90% in many European countries), relatively short in duration (six to nine months compared to one to three years in many European countries), and relatively restrictively granted. In the United States about 60% of the unemployed receive no benefits because of ineligibility. The after-tax average replacement ratio of those who do is estimated, by Clark and Summers (1979), to be 66%. In Europe the number of beneficiaries of unemployment benefits is not much different from the number of unemployed revealed by labor force surveys. The main reason for the relatively low coverage of the unemployed in the United States is the short duration of the benefits. Longer-term unemployed fall outside the reach of unemployment compensation. Unemployment benefits are even of unlimited duration in some European countries, such as Belgium and Germany, where the benefits are somewhat lower after a year. In addition, the long-term unemployed in Europe benefit from a number of other income-maintenance programs.

The costs of unemployment compensation to public budgets ranged in 1981 from small amounts (0.5% of GDP or less in the United States, Japan, Sweden, and Switzerland) to 1.5–2% of GDP in Germany, France, and the United Kingdom, to 2.5–3.5% of GDP in Belgium and Denmark (see table 3.5 in a later section). These amounts were certainly considerably higher by 1986 in most of the European countries, with unemployment at 11% on average, compared to 8% in 1981.

Sickness Benefits

A clear-cut difference between the United States and Europe is that in the United States there is no national scheme and few state schemes (six states in all) for paying sickness benefits to workers absent for reasons of ill health, whereas in Europe benefits are given at least at the level of unemployment benefits and sometimes higher. State benefits in Germany and Sweden are 80% and 90% of pay, respectively, and in France and Italy collective bargaining agreements often ensure considerably higher compensation than the state benefits. Most European countries provide between 60% and 90% compensation from social security funds after an uncompensated waiting period of up to three days. However, Germany requires the employer to pay sickness benefits for the first six weeks.

As shown in table 3.2, in the United States the average yearly absence because of ill health was five days in 1981, compared to sixteen days in the largest four European countries on average. In the United States there is little or no cost to the public budget. In Europe the total cost to the economy of absenteeism beyond the low American level (that is, sixteen days less five days) amounts to about 5% of total labor costs. Of this a substantial fraction is borne by public funds. Losses of working time because of illness are incomparably greater than those resulting from strikes. In Italy and the United Kingdom, where strikes have been heaviest among European countries, less than one day per year per employee has been lost because of strikes in the period 1980–1985 (Bureau of Labor Statistics, 1985).

The relationship between the generosity of the benefits and the rate of absenteeism can hardly be ignored. Moreover, there is abundant information about abuse of sickness benefit schemes, for example, the ease with which medical certificates can be obtained and the coincidence of high absenteeism on days before or after weekends or public holidays. In 1984 in Italy, for example, it was necessary to issue a directive requiring beneficiaries of sick pay to be at home, if not in the hospital, available for possible visits by an inspector.

Table 3.2
Absenteesim from work because of ill health (days per year)

Country	1960	1970	1981
United States	5.6	5.4	4.9
France	13.2	13.3	14.9
Germany	13.9	13.1	12.3
Italy	–	12.7	17.2[a]
United Kingdom	13.8	16.7	20.0
Belgium	17.2	21.6	21.3[b]
The Netherlands	5.3	7.7	8.5
Norway	9.9	11.4	–
Finland	–	–	3.6
Sweden	13.2	19.9	19.6
Austria	19.6	18.0	17.1
Ireland	19.5	25.6	33.8[b]
Greece	5.6	5.0	5.8[b]
Portugal	–	–	4.5[b]

Source: OECD (1986).
a. 1975
b. 1980

Invalidity and Disability Pensions

Invalidity and disability pensions have greatly expanded in many countries. In the United States, Japan, and Europe disability pensions (granted to victims of work injury) usually have the highest benefit ceilings, often 80–100% of prior earnings for those suffering total disability. Invalidity pensions (granted as a result of permanent illness or reduced capacity to work) are typically at the same level as the state old-age pension.

Data on the number of beneficiaries, supplied by officials of national adminstrations to an international conference on disability in 1986 (Yates 1986), are given in table 3.3. The data suggest, as a rule of thumb, the following distinction between two groups of countries. On the one hand, some countries have kept such programs relatively closely confined to people with important medical disabilities, in which case the number may be about $3\frac{1}{2}\%$ in relation to total employment (United States, United Kingdom). On the other hand, a second group

Table 3.3
Number of beneficiaries of disability pensions

Country	1970 (thousands)	1975 (thousands)	1983 (thousands)	1983 (% of employed)
United States[a]	2,587	4,129	3,865	3.5
Germany[a]	1,621	1,746	2,332	10
United Kingdom[a]	–	450	737	3.5
The Netherlands[b]	237	344	673	12.0
Finland[b]	50	169	171	5.0
Sweden[b]	177	263	301	6.3
Austria[a]	288	284	357	12

Source: Yates (1986).
a. Persons benfiting from full disability pensions.
b. Persons benefiting from full and partial disability pensions, of which full pensions account for 80–90% of the total.

of countries has expanded the disability programs massively into programs of long-term unemployment compensation for elderly workers who have difficulties obtaining suitable jobs, such pensioners perhaps but not necessarily having some medical problems. These countries, including Austria, Germany, Italy, the Netherlands, and Sweden, have seen the number of "disability" pensions rise to 10% or more in relation to total employment. This number is, of course, large in relation to total unemployment. Italy (not covered in the source for table 3.3) has the highest number of all: 29% in relation to total employment in 1978 (Haveman et al. 1984).

Another way of giving perspective to the expansion of disability pensions beyond the initial program objectives is to express the number of beneficiaries as a percentage of the number of old-age pensioners. In 1983 this percentage was a minimal 8% in the United Kingdom and 16% in the United States. The percentage rises to 21% in Sweden, 36% in Germany, and 48% in the Netherlands (Yates 1986). In Italy the national percentage was 43% in 1978 (more recent data are lacking), but in the Mezzogiorno the figure was 250%, and in the Enna district of Sicily it was 669% (Vitali 1984). In the south of Italy the program has clearly become a regional one for ensuring permanent income maintenance of a high level for the unemployed. Many of these people live in mountain villages and towns with little agricultural, industrial, or commerical potential. The local economy is a pension economy, but unlike many other pension economies, such as on the southern coasts of England, France, and the United States, this one has a preponderance of pensioners of preretirement age.

The main reasons for the enormous growth of disability pensions in the last fifteen years can be traced to changes in eligibility criteria, which have become more heavily weighted by social and economic factors rather than by strictly medical factors (Haveman et al. 1984). In Germany court decisions between 1969 and 1976 introduced absence of "an appropriate job" as a more important criterion. In Italy legislation in 1969 introduced the worker's social and economic environment as a criterion. In the Netherlands the existence of employment opportunities was introduced as a criterion in 1973, and the assumed degree of handicap was also increased. In Sweden workers over 60, from the early 1970s on, no longer had to undergo a medical test if their employment prospects were bad, and employers welcomed this as a way of reducing the constraints imposed by the law on dismissal of redundant staff. The United States also introduced in the early 1970s the criterion of nonmedical impairment of capacity to achieve vocational standards.

Data on the total of benefits paid for invalidity, disability, and work injury for European Community countries show the range rising from 1.2% to 2.7% of GDP in 1970 to 1.8% to 6.1% of GDP in 1983. In the Netherlands the increase was from 2.3% to 6.1% of GDP. These amounts are now for most countries as high as those for unemployment benefits and, in the Netherlands and Italy, considerably higher (see table 3.4).

Table 3.4
Invalidity, disability, and work injury benefits, % GDP

Country	1970	1980	1983
France	1.8	2.2	2.4
Germany	2.5	3.2	3.2
Italy	—	4.7	5.5
United Kingdom	1.4	2.1	2.3
Belgium	2.2	3.8	3.5
The Netherlands	2.3	5.8	6.1
Denmark	2.7	2.5	2.6
Ireland	1.2	1.5	1.8

Source: Commission of the European Communities (Eurostat) (1985a).

Early Retirement Pensions

A related type of program for withdrawing surplus workers from the labor force and the unemployment register lies in the granting of early retirement pensions [see Carrol and Tamburi (1985) for details]. The minimum age is usually set around two to five years below the normal retirement age, with a replacement income typically of 60% to 80% assured until the regular pension becomes available. Countries having made important use of such schemes include Germany, France, the United Kingdom, Belgium, and Denmark. Their function is in several cases hardly different from that of the greatly expanded disability pension schemes. However, early retirement schemes are of several types, even in single countries. Some are linked to the filling of a vacancy by an unemployed young person and are heavily subsidized (Belgium, France, Germany, United Kingdom). Some are actuarily more neutral schemes offering a flexible choice of retirement age (Belgium, France, Spain, Sweden). Others in effect overlap with disability programs (Denmark, Germany, Sweden). Some are reserved for long-term unemployed workers reaching a certain age, usually between 56 and 60 (Belgium, France, Germany, the Netherlands, Sweden, Spain, the United Kingdom). The number of people and costs involved is in some cases quite considerable. The fraction of total pensions paid to those under the normal retirement age was 8% in Belgium in 1984, 11% in Denmark in 1984, 14% in France in 1982 (before measures to reduce the retirement age from 65 to 60), and 20% in Germany in 1985. Expenditures on early retirement pensions would in these cases range from about 1% to 2% of GDP. It has been reported in a number of social and psychological surveys that there is little or no difference between the incidence of psychological problems among the unemployed and the early retired. All the countries experimenting with these schemes have taken care to give them only a temporary life, so as to make them reversible and to prevent them from becoming a normally expected option for older workers.

Invalidity pensioners and early retirees have thus come to represent in large measure an additional army of unemployed persons. This increase has been the result of the same factors that caused the official unemployment register to rise (weak demand, high labor costs, weak profits and investment). However, they do not contribute to any automatic adjustment in the economy that might help increase employment. On the contrary, in being subtracted from the labor supply and having a motivation to work, they dampen pressure on the real wage level to adjust to the labor market disequilibrium. In addition, they have added substantially to social security costs and therefore to total labor costs and so caused a further reduction in labor demand.

In 1986 the Dutch government decided on an extensive program of policy reforms designed to reduce the enormous cost of its existing disability programs. These measures are listed as an example of the numerous variables that can be adjusted in an effort to cut costs. The basic full disability and unemployment benefit level was reduced from 80% to 70% of prior income. In the future only medical and vocational criteria will be used for deciding on pensions. A wider range of jobs in a wider geographical area will be taken into account in reviewing the vocational criteria. The condition of the labor market will no longer influence the judgment of degree of disability. Cases of partial disability and partial unemployment will no longer be treated as cases of complete disability. The unemployment benefit will be reduced over time from 70% of prior earnings to 70% of the minimum wage in half-yearly steps. Existing beneficiaries of disability pensions will be rescreened in 1986 if under 30 years of age, and possibly in subsequent years if aged between 30 and 50 years. Italy and Spain have also begun to rescreen existing beneficiaries of disability pensions.

Family and Maternity Benefits

Family and maternity benefits do not exist in the United States, whereas they are standard in Europe, generally costing between 2% and 3% of GDP (see table 3.5) in European Community countries. In the United States, as in Europe, income tax allowances are granted because of family commitments, but the value of these concessions is significant only for those with sufficiently high taxable income. In Europe family benefits, generally granted without income tests, are a significant source of income maintenance for low-income and unemployed people.

The relative stability of the percentage amounts of GDP granted in family and maternity benefits over time from 1970 to 1983 no doubt reflects the clear-cut nature of the elegibility criteria and ease of administrative control, contrasting, for example, with sickness and disability benefits. There also appears to have been a convergence in benefit levels among countries, with Belgium remaining the most generous country, although relatively less so than in earlier years. Despite several years of budgetary austerity, Belgian benefits still contain a

Table 3.5
Family and maternity benefits, % GDP

Country	1970	1980	1983
France	3.0	3.1	3.1
Germany	2.1	2.3	2.1
Italy	—	1.6	2.0
United Kingdom	1.6	2.7	2.8
Belgium	3.5	3.3	3.2
The Netherlands	2.8	2.8	2.8
Denmark	2.7	3.3	3.1
Ireland	2.1	2.3	3.0

Source: Commission of the European Communities (Eurostat) (1985a).

number of uniquely generous features, such as a substantial holiday allowance paid to all workers in mid-summer. The origin of this system was no doubt to ensure that all workers could afford to take a family holiday. However, because Belgian salaries are among the highest in the world, the objective justification for this scheme is no longer so evident.

Other Income-Maintenance Programs

The remaining categories of income maintenance are often means-tested programs. Many European countries have programs of supplementary family benefits (Italy, United Kingdom) or minimum family income granted in relation to an income test (France, Belgium), and in some cases these grants are based on further administratively judged criteria of need (Sweden). Some European countries, however, rely mainly on unemployment assistance grants, which are usually means tested and come into effect when normal unemployment benefits expire (Germany, Austria, the Netherlands, Finland). The United States has means-tested benefits, mainly for one-parent families and through food stamps.

The essential difference between the typical European income-maintenance system and that of the United States lies not so much in these residual means-tested programs but in the extent of non-means-tested programs, such as child benefits. A detailed study by Rainwater et al. (1986), covering Sweden, the United Kingdom, and the United States, showed some relatively similar effects from their respective means-tested programs. In each case about half of the poor people (those with incomes below half the median income) received such benefits. In each of the three countries about one-third of these recipients were lifted above the poverty line. The main difference lies in the number of people who were below the poverty line before the application of the means-tested benefits: 3.1% of the population in Sweden, 5.4% in the United Kingdom, and 15.5% in the United States. Because similar percentage shares of these groups were then lifted above the poverty line through means-tested benefits, clearly the number remaining below the poverty line in the United States was much greater (see section 3.4).

The problem of unemployment in Europe is far worse that the already high figure of 11% of the labor force who receive unemployment benefits in 1986. Most European countries have effective unemployment rates in the range of 15% to 25%, if one also adds the number of early retired pensioners and the increase in the number of disability pensioners beyond those covered by serious medical incapacity. These aggregate unemployment rates are in fact probably more similar than the official unemployment statistics suggest. Germany has much expanded its disability/early retirement scheme; Italy and the Netherlands have expanded their disability schemes; Belgium, France, and the United Kingdom, their early retirement schemes, and Sweden, both disability and early retirement schemes.

The cost to social security budgets of these three programs—unemployment benefits, early retirement pensions, and extended "disability" pensions—is of considerable macroeconomic significance: probably 5% of GDP in most European countries and approaching 10% in some. When family benefits and sickness compensation are added, most European countries are spending around 10% of GDP on transfer payments to people of working age, which translates into an addition to wage costs of the order of 20%. The United States, Japan, and Switzerland are paying only a small fraction of these sums on such programs. Indeed, in some cases the programs do not exist at all, as in the case of family and sickness benefits in the United States.

In the event of a successful strategy in Europe to return to a high-employment society, a large fraction of expenditures on welfare programs would wither away. In the course of so doing, social security taxes could be greatly reduced and the expansion of employment further boosted. Unlike expenditure on basic social services discussed in the next section (health care, education, pensions), high expenditure on transfer payments to the unemployed is the mark of an unsuccessful society. A broad strategy to move back to a high-employment society, involving both supply and demand sides of economic policy, is outlined in chapter 4. In the meantime the closing paragraphs of this section identify some of the policy reforms that could be envisaged for individual income-maintenance programs as part of such a strategy.

1. High unemployment compensation is justified for an initial period of unemployment, say up to a year. As the duration of unemployment lengthens, the level of benefits should reduce substantially and pressures to accept available jobs, including public work schemes, should be increased. To help reemployment, reduced social security contributions should be charged on enterprises recruiting a long-term unemployed person. Many countries have such features in their present schemes, but these could be accentuated as part of a broader employment growth strategy, including appropriately expansionary macroeconomic policy.

2. Sickness benefits (that is, compensation for pay lost during absence from work) should be tightened in many countries. The burden of control is carried by the employer. The state's contribution to sickness benefits could in many countries be substantially reduced, as could the related payroll taxes. The enterprise would have a stronger role in controlling abuse.

3. Invalidity and disability pensions should revert to their proper role of covering strictly medical problems, to the exclusion of economic criteria. New pensions should thus be awarded much more restrictively than in the past in many European countries. Because a large part of this population is relatively old, the number of beneficiaries of such programs would revert relatively quickly to a normal size. In addition, there is the more

delicate question of how acquired rights should be treated. Italy and the Netherlands have initiated programs for reexamining the degree of disability of those presently covered, especially those who are not old. The percentage degree of disability could be reassessed where total disability pensions have been granted for minor medical handicaps. Help should be extended for these people to become employed again, for example, with reduced social security changes.

4. Extreme generosity in some countries in various family benefits could cut back, for example, the substantial holiday allowance that remains in Belgium despite years of negotiations over the trimming of other public expenditures.

5. Early retirement schemes should be phased out as part of a return to a high-employment society. Employment of relatively elderly people, often on a part-time basis, should be encouraged, for example, through easier conditions of recruitment and dismissal and reduced social security changes (as in Japan, which has an important employment subsidy scheme for near-retirement workers). Policy for normal pensions faces its own crisis in the years ahead for demographic reasons, but this is a separate matter (see section 3.4).

3.4   Basic Social Services

Everyone needs health care, education, and pensions. There is a positive correlation between the demand for such services and income level. There are also positive relationships between productive capacity and good health, education, and the supply of savings associated with pension provisions. These core social services thus distinguish themselves from several income-maintenance programs, the expanded use of which indicates failures in the economic and social system. It is not surprising, therefore, that there is less variance among countries in the share of resources that are devoted to the core social services rather than to income-maintenance programs. Public expenditures on these three programs in many countries cost around 5–7% of GDP each. This is a relatively narrow range by comparison with income-maintenance programs that cost as little as 1% of GDP in Switzerland and as high as 16% of GDP in Belgium (table 3.6).

With health, education, and pension expenditures by the public sector usually amounting to 15–20% of GDP, there arise correspondingly important issues of policy design and management. A thorough discussion of these issues requires books, rather than a few pages. The following limited remarks are therefore addressed to the particular question of whether there are basic questions of policy regime that deserve to be opened up and, in particular, whether the European social model in these areas needs to be reconsidered.

Health Care

One main question of regime choice concerns the degree of public versus private provision of health care, education, and pensions. This question turns on three main subissues: (1) the impact of the tax burden on macroeconomic variables, such as wages, employment, and investment; (2) the efficiency of expenditure systems in achieving the direct objectives of health, education, and pension provision; and (3) implications for the equity of society.

In the health care field the primary categorization of regimes among the industrialized countries is between the United States and the rest of the European countries and Japan. The United States is unique in having no universal public health care system and only partial systems covering retired people (Medicare) and poor families (Medicaid). Apart from these categories, which in 1985 covered 50 million out of 238 million people, there is the option of buying private insurance, if the individuals or their employers are able and willing to do so, or remaining uninsured or substantially underinsured. In 1977, 18 million people were

Table 3.6
Share of social expenditures in % GDP, 1981[a]

Country	Education	Health	Pensions[b]	Unemployment	Other social expenditure[c]	Total social expenditure
United States	5.5	4.2	7.4	0.5	3.2	20.8
Japan	5.0	4.7	4.8	0.4	2.6	17.5
France	5.7	6.5	11.9	1.9	3.5	29.5
Germany	5.2	6.5	12.5	1.4	5.9	31.5
Italy	6.4	6.0	13.2	0.7	2.8	29.1
United Kingdom	5.8	5.4	7.4	1.4	3.7	23.7
Belgium	7.9	5.1	9.1	2.6	13.5	38.3
The Netherlands	7.1	6.7	13.0	1.0	8.3	36.1
Denmark	7.7	5.6	7.5	3.4	8.8	33.4
Finland	6.3	5.2	8.8	0.6	4.0	25.9
Sweden	6.6	8.9	11.8	0.5	6.1	33.4
Switzerland	5.5	5.4	8.3	0.1	0.9	20.1
Austria	3.8	4.7	13.9	0.5	4.9	27.9
Greece	2.4	3.5	5.7	0.3	1.5	13.4

Source: OECD (1985c).
a. 1980 for Belgium and Greece, 1979 for Denmark and Switzerland.
b. Including disability benefits.
c. Expenditure on sickness, maternity, temporary disability, family and child allowances, and other social assistance and welfare services.

completely uncovered by public or private insurance during the whole year, and another 18 million were uncovered during part of the year (Davis and Rowland 1983). These people are principally among the unemployed and poorer sections of the community, with some concentration on ethnic minorities. Eligibility of people of working age for public health care (under Medicaid) is attached to an income test of variable height by state, ranging from the extraordinarily low level of $89 per month in Alabama to $508 per month in Alaska. The number of those falling below the official poverty standard of $397 per month who are eligible for Medicaid is only 50% for twenty-one states mainly in the South and West, whereas it is over 90% in eight states, including Massachusetts and California.

The high degree of privatization of the supply and financing of health care in the United States has led to the following advantages and disadvantages. The physical availability of health care of the highest technical standard is ensured for those who can pay and without rationing, as manifested in other countries by queues and waiting lists. But the lack of availability for people with limited or no insurance is often a real and dramatic problem. The objective of reasonable equity—the assurance for all the population of health care of basic quality or for catastrophic illnesses—is far from being attained. It is also apparent that, despite various managerial initiatives, such as health maintenance organizations, the costs of health care have been poorly controlled for a variety of reasons. Some point to the absence of adequate powers to control the American Medical Assoiation in the public interest. Many analysts point to the weakness of incentives for cost control in many private insurance systems. The extreme extension of private market rules in the health system also appear to be responsible for some ugly abuses, such as the extent of suing for malpractice and the cost for the medical profession and the patient of insuring against malpractice suits (for example, obstetricians and surgeons reportedly have to pay $50,000 or more per year in malpractice insurance premiums).

General indicators of health standards and of delivered health care point to a ranking of the United States in the same league as the other industrialized countries. Life expectancy in the United States is basically the same as in Japan and Western Europe. Infant mortality is the same in the United States and Western Europe but lower in Japan. The average length of use of hospitals on an in-patient basis and the number of hospital beds is about half in the United States what it is in Japan and Western Europe, no doubt because of the extremely high costs of hospitalization in the United States and the extent of patient cost participation. The share of GDP accounted for by total expenditures on health care is, however, significantly higher in the United States (10.8%) compared to Europe (7.8%) or Japan (6.7%). The split between public and private financing is, as already stressed, quite different: 42% public to 58% private in the United States, 80% public to 20% private in Europe and Japan. Most European countries are able to provide universal health care of good to high quality for between 7% and 9% of GDP from a combination of public and private financing. Severe compression of public health services, as in the United Kingdom, where rationing through long hospital waiting lists is common, is associated in that country with considerable parsimony on total health expenditure (6.2% of a relatively low GDP in the United Kingdom, compared to 7.8% of a higher GDP in Europe on average).

Private financing of health care in Europe averages 1.2% of GDP and is of the same level in Japan. This degree of private financing largely consists of cost sharing by the patient in the case of noncatastrophic treatment, for dentistry, medications, consultations, and hospitalization charges.

The lower share of public financing of health care in the United States contributes to lower social security taxes. However, private health insurance is then an additional cost for employer and employee, and this is borne out in data on the relative size of private fringe costs of employment. In 1981 nonobligatory social welfare costs averaged 9% of total labor costs in the United States, compared to 3% in Germany (Hart 1984). Eighty percent of employees of medium- to large-sized American companies benefit from private health insurance (OECD 1985c). We doubt that employees in wage bargaining or employers in their propensity to take on staff behave differently depending on whether a given amount of health insurance is paid for through private or public schemes. Arguments that rely on the contribution of social security taxes to labor costs and from there to a dampening of the demand for labor may not take into account the alternative private costs of health expenditure or pensions that would have occurred otherwise and hence can be exaggerated.

Education

As regards education expenditure, there is no prima facie case for suggesting that the policy regimes in Europe have gone badly astray or that they have contributed to an exaggerated expansion of the public sector and tax burdens. The range of educational spending as a share of GDP is quite narrow among the larger industrialized countries (5.0% in Japan, 5.5% in the United States and the largest four European countries). Private schooling is a small fraction of the total in all countries. The quality of public schooling is a major issue in the United States, where the functional illiteracy rates of school leavers is astonishingly high [between 8% and 20% depending on the severity of the literacy test; see Thurow (1985c)]. A Census Bureau study in 1986 found that 13% of US adults are illiterate (*New York Times*, April 21, 1986). The 1986 Carnegie report on the teaching profession draws attention to the low level of teacher's pay and academic standards (*New York Times*, May 16, 1986). Public school teachers in the United States earn on average less than mail carriers and only a little more than secretaries. Tests of international schooling standards quoted by Thurow show functional illiteracy to be slight in Europe and Japan and achievement levels to be higher, especially in mathematics in Japan. Reduced expenditure on state schooling in the United Kingdom has, however, caused serious quality problems there. The hypothesis of more extensive private schooling is not a major issue in most countries because of the problems of inequity and insufficiency of the basic national educational standard that would be implied.

In higher education the issue of private financing poses itself in somewhat different terms. The benefits of university education accrue to the individual, and the practicability of students earning some money and contracting loans to be repaid after their studies is demonstrated, notably in the United States. The issue of equity is not in this case quite the same problem that it is for privately funded schooling for children. The United States model has, in this sector, therefore, a number of features that could be attractive to other countries concerned with the budgetary burden of university education. In the United States the funding of university education is broken down as follows: public subsidies, 46%; fees and costs borne by students (or parents), 33%; and other private sources, 21%. Officially guaranteed student loans account for one-third of the fees and costs borne by students. The fees and costs borne by students was $24 billion, or 0.7% of GDP, in 1981–1982 (National Center for Education Statistics, 1985).

Comparable data are not available for Europe, but the share of public subsidies is certainly much higher and the share of private sources much smaller. Student loans were introduced to replace grants in Germany in 1982 but are not common elsewhere in Europe. Their possible introduction is under consideration in the United Kingdom. One indicator of the extent of income earned by students working on a part-time basis is provided by data on the part-time employment of young people. In the United States $5\frac{1}{2}$ million young people under the age of 24 held part-time jobs in 1983, whereas in the same year in the European Community the comparable figure was under 2 million [Bureau of Labor Statistics, 1986; Comission of the European Communities (Eurostat), 1985b]. However, a substantial increase in the volume of student part-time work in Europe would require considerable changes in employment regulations of the type already discussed, for example, greater freedom of employers to take on temporary or short-term and part-time staff. Lower social security contribution rates for young people, such as those introduced already in some European countries, would also be helpful in further boosting demand for student jobs.

Pensions

Important differences in public pension schemes depend on how far the public sector goes beyond providing a minimal flat-rate universal pension toward providing a fully earnings-related pension. A typical public pension nowadays offers about a 66% replacement ratio by comparison with the beneficiary's income a few years before retirement. This was exactly the United States figure in 1980, whereas that of Japan was 61%. Both countries made large upward revisions of their replacement ratios in the 1970s, from around 40% in 1969 (see table 3.7). In Europe in 1980 the average replacement ratio was 62%, which also marked an upward revision during the period since 1969, but by a much smaller margin because the average European replacement ratio was then already 54%. Thus the broad picture for the last fifteen years is one in which the United States, Japan, and Europe have tended to converge in their public pension systems. The United States and Japan have increased their public pensions fastest and lifted them to the highest levels.

The European situation, however, is characterized by much

Table 3.7
Repacement rates of social security old-age pensions for workers with average wages in manufacturing, for couples, 1969–1980

| Country | Pension as percent of earnings in year before retirement | | System type |
	1969	1980	
United States	44	66	earnings-related pension
Japan	39	61	two-part formula
France	56	75	earnings-related pension
Germany	55	49	earnings-related pension
Italy	62	69	earnings-related pension
United Kingdom	43	47	two-tier pension
The Netherlands	61	63	flat-rate pension
Denmark	45	52	two-tier pension
Sweden	56	83	two-tier pension
Austria	87	68	earnings-related pension
Switzerland	45	55	two-part formula

Source: Aldrich (1982).

wider divergences in national pension systems than in most social policies. The replacement ratios of public pensions range from low levels of 47–49% in the United Kingdom and Germany, to 69% in Italy, 75% in France, and even 83% in Sweden.

When public pensions exceed about 66% of prior income, it seems justified to raise questions of whether the pension level has not been raised unnecessarily high. The average retired household, to maintain its preretirement consumption level, needs considerably less than its peak earnings level before retirement. Expenses of child rearing, education, and primary residence purchase are normally over. Personal savings are typically accumulated during the second half of a working career and used for consumption in retirement. Where the retirement pension is particularly high, the incentive to make private sav-

Table 3.8
Projections of the share of elderly in the population and pensions
expenditure on unchanged policies

Country	% Share of elderly in total population			Share of public pension expenditure in GDP, unchanged policies		
	1980	2010	2040	1980	2010	2040
United States	11.3	12.8	19.8	8.3	8.7	14.9
Japan	9.1	18.6	22.7	6.0	12.3	15.7
France	14.0	16.3	22.7	14.3	17.4	27.1
Germany	15.5	20.4	27.6	13.8	19.8	31.2
Italy	13.5	17.3	24.2	16.6	22.0	35.1
United Kingdom	14.9	14.6	20.4	7.8	7.6	11.4
European Community (4)	14.5	17.1	23.7	13.8	16.7	26.2
Belgium	14.4	15.9	21.9	14.1	14.9	22.8
The Netherlands	11.5	15.1	24.8	12.2	15.2	28.8
Sweden	16.3	17.5	22.5	13.0	12.9	18.1
Spain	10.9	15.5	22.7	9.5	11.7	19.4

Source: OECD, 1986b.
See note to table 3.9 for definitions.

ings during working years will be low, and the incentive to
stop work completely on reaching pensionable age may be
undesirably high by economic and social criteria.

The major issue of pension policy for the years ahead is how
to adapt to profound changes in demographic structure. Aging
of the population over the next fifty years is going to be
common to all industrialized countries (see table 3.8). From
1980 to 2040 the United States will see its share of elderly
(65 and older) in the population grow from 11% to 19%. In
Japan the increase will be even steeper, from 9% to 23%. In
Europe the increase will average from 15% to 24%. On unchanged policies (constant retirement age and indexation provisions) the amount of public expenditure on pensions would be
expected, according to OECD calculations, to rise from 8% to

Table 3.9
Projections of pensions expenditure on unchanged and changed policies

Country	1980	2000	2025
Pensions expenditure in % GDP under unchanged policies, benefits indexed on gross earnings.			
United States	4.2	4.7	7.4
Japan	3.4	6.0	10.4
Germany	7.8	9.1	13.7
United Kingdom	4.4	4.9	7.2
Pensions expenditure in GDP with a one-year increase in the pension age each five years from 1995 to 2015 (e.g., rising from 65 to 70), with benefits indexed on net earnings.			
United States	4.2	4.3	5.6
Japan	3.4	5.4	8.6
Germany	7.8	7.9	9.7
United Kingdom	4.4	4.5	5.7

Source: Halter and Hemming (1985).
Halter and Hemming (1985) use a narrow definition of old-age benefits compared to the OECD study quoted in table 3.8. The OECD study includes disability and survivors' pensions paid to the elderly, as well as some other transfer programs, such as minimum guaranteed income for the elderly, and some special allowances (housing, attendance allowance, etc.). Halter and Hemming also exclude benefits to public employees.

15% of GDP in the United States, from 6% to 16% in Japan, and from 15% to 30% of GDP on average in France, Germany, and Italy (see table 3.8). Estimates by Halter and Hemming (1985) of the IMF (in table 3.9) also indicate substantial increases in pension expenditures on unchanged policies, although the levels are lower (definitional coverage is narrower, as explained in the note to table 3.9, and the time horizon of the projections is shorter).

The larger part of these projected increases in pension expenditure occurs in the years 2000 to 2040, which explains the policy reaction in the United States: to raise the retirement age progressively from 65 to 67 between 2000 and 2017. In this way the United States can eliminate the looming deficit of its social security trust funds (Pechman 1986).

In Europe it is yet to be decided in many countries how to avoid an economically unbearable rise in pension costs. There can be no doubt that the cost of maintaining present pensions policies, for example, as projected in table 3.8, would impose impossibly large additional taxation, perhaps as much as 30% increases in the payroll tax on employment. In the simplest terms there are three options to avoid this crippling rise in taxation: (1) cut the pension benefit as a percentage of prior income, (2) raise the retirement age, and (3) raise taxation in some degree in a compromise solution.

Some of the industrialized contries have already made some policy reforms to correct for these unsustainable trends. The United States has made some tax increases and deferral of benefit increases. This is in addition to lowering early retirement benefits, increasing delayed retirement credits, and, as already noted, increasing the future retirement age. Germany has so far relied on reductions in the replacement ratio of pension to prior earnings. As was indicated in table 3.7, Germany's pension replacement ratio of 49% is now one of the lowest of all the industrialized countries. However, its pension system has certainly not yet been rendered sustainable for the first half of the twenty-first century, and further tax rises or pension cuts would seem increasingly difficult. The United Kingdom government sought in 1985 to eliminate prospective financial imbalance in its earnings-related pension supplement by privatization, thus switching this pension component from a public pay-as-you-go fund to private and fully funded pension schemes. Political support was not obtained, however, to make this change in its entirety. Switching to a fully funded pension scheme could imply substantially changing the savings-consumption balance of the economy and therefore possibly the need to sustain large balance-of-payment current account surpluses of the kind at present seen in Germany and Japan.

This poses serious questions of feasibility as the number of countries in this situation grows, and problems of trade and industrial imbalances could prove difficult to manage.

Given the high level of taxation in Europe, it may be argued that the broad thrust of pension policy reform should go more in the direction of gradually raising the retirement age and gradually lowering benefit levels in countries where these are at relatively high levels. The recent United States reform, gradually extending the retirement age in the early decades of the next century, has much to commend it. Transposed into a European setting, this reform would further intensify the need for labor market measures to help older people to be employed in ways suitable to their tastes and capacities. Because the working capacity of elderly people is mixed, a flexible retirement age would be desirable. The United Kingdom government has recently advanced the concept of making the sixties a decade of retirement; that is, retirement should be an option from the ages of 60 to 70, with neutral financial incentives, however, to avoid a bunching of retirement in the early sixties. Halter and Hemming (1985) have made some calculations of the financial savings to be made in pensions in the event of raising the retirement age (see table 3.9). A large contribution to solving the problem of soaring pensions expenditures could be obtained in this way.

In Europe sound management rather than fundamental changes in policy regimes is what appears to be called for in the case of the core social services such as health care, education, and the provision of pensions.

In these policy domains the extreme critique that Europe has been overindulging in the welfare state at the cost of its employment and productive potential does not seem founded.

1. In the health care domain the highly privatized United States has larger problems of basic policy design to resolve than Europe or Japan. This of course still leaves many important

management challenges for health policy in Europe. User charges for noncatastrophic medical costs and a small but growing privately financed health sector will no doubt continue to figure in the difficult task of reconciling conflicts among supply, demand, and equity in Europe. But the case for massive privatization of medicine seems weak. In the United States problems resulting from excessive privatization of the financing of health care appear to be far more serious.

2. Similarly, in the domain of education there is no evidence that Europe has overindulged in public expenditure, although some adjustments may now be made for changing demographic structures. There are some opportunities for transferring more of higher education costs to beneficiaries, with positive features to be seen in the United States system of student loans and part-time employment. The often unsatisfactory quality of public schooling in the United States and the United Kingdom stands out as a major problem.

3. Changing demographic structures, with more elderly and fewer working-age people, are posing acute issues for public pensions policy that stretch from now well into the twenty-first century. These policy issues are probably severest for Japan, followed by Europe and then the United States. Such measures as raising the retirement age look increasingly relevant, although benefits may also have to be reduced in some European countries. The privatization of pension contributions does not appear to be a particularly interesting policy option in this regard.

3.5   Poverty and Income Redistribution: The Overall Results

It is generally recognized that Western Europe has a more extensive system of welfare benefits and income maintenance than the United States. The cost in terms of higher taxation and social security contribution rates is transparent. The impact on income equality is not so self-evident. Critics of Europe's welfare systems suggest that the profusion of overlapping benefits tends toward a redistribution from everybody to everybody: a massive diminution of incentives to work, combined with less than satisfactory results in terms of eliminating poverty. On the other side of the Atlantic critics of the Reagan adminstration's cuts in welfare expenditures argue that the United States's relatively unequal income distribution is becoming even more unequal.

New evidence on comparative income distribution and poverty in seven countries comes from the Luxembourg Income Study (O'Higgins et al. 1985), which assembled and analyzed comparable income and demographic survey results. A large data bank has been set up, containing for each country forty-two income and wage variables combined with thirty-five sociodemographic variables for each country (see table 3.10 for sources).

Studies of poverty are bedeviled as much by the complexity and obscurity of different measures of inequality as by the dearth of information. The Luxembourg Income Study gives prominence to rather simple and transparent criteria. They focus attention on the pre- and posttax and transfer income situation of the quintiles of the income distribution hierarchy, with family income per head taken as the basic measure. The data presented in table 3.10 are for 1979; they are ranked by income and given in percentages of the population whose incomes fall *below one-half of the median income level of the population*. Poverty is defined in these terms.

In the United States, Germany, and the United Kingdom there was a striking similarity in 1979 in the percentage of people who were poor in terms of their incomes before public transfers and taxes. In all three cases about 27–28% of the population had gross incomes lower than half the median income. After taxes and transfers this percentage falls to 17% in the United States, a reduction by a little over one-third in the

Table 3.10
Pre- and posttransfer poverty rates in 1979[a]

| Country[b] | Percentage of persons who are poor in | | | | |
	Elderly families	Single-parent families	Two-parent families	Other families	Total
United States					
Pretransfer	72.0	58.5	16.0	15.4	27.3
Posttransfer	20.5	51.7	12.9	9.8	16.9
Percent reduction	−71.5	−11.6	−19.4	−36.4	−38.1
Germany					
Pretransfer	80.3	34.8	12.9	20.1	28.3
Posttransfer	9.3	18.1	3.9	5.4	6.0
Percent reduction	−88.4	−47.1	−69.8	−73.1	−78.8
United Kingdom					
Pretransfer	78.6	56.3	17.6	12.8	27.9
Posttransfer	18.1	29.1	6.5	4.1	8.8
Percent reduction	−77.0	−48.3	−63.1	−68.0	−68.5
Sweden					
Pretransfer	98.4	55.0	21.3	30.5	41.0
Posttransfer	0.1	9.2	5.0	7.0	5.0
Percent reduction	−99.9	−83.3	−76.5	−77.0	−87.8
Norway					
Pretransfer	76.9	44.0	7.7	18.7	24.1
Posttransfer	4.6	12.6	3.4	5.7	4.8
Percent reduction	−94.0	−71.4	−56.4	−69.5	−80.1

Source: Smeeding et al. (1985).
a. Poverty is defined as family income of below half the median income level.
b. The data sets and their sample size for countries relevant to the present study are: the US Current Population Survey, 1979 (69,000); the UK Family Expenditure Survey, 1979 (6,900); the German Transfer Survey, 1979 (9,600); the Swedish Income Distribution and Level of Living Survey, 1979 (9,600); the Norwegian Tax Files, 1979 (10,400). The methodology and basic statistical results are given in O'Higgins et al. (1985).

number of poor people. In Germany and the United Kingdom the percentage falls to 6% and 9%, respectively, which amounts to a reduction of poverty of twice the amplitude seen in the United States.

Germany and the United Kingdom represent the middle ground among European welfare state models in terms of the size of government measured by taxes and public expenditures as a share of GDP. Sweden and Norway represent the most extensive welfare states. In the Scandinavian countries the post-tax and transfer situation of the poor is improved a little more than in Germany and the United Kingdom; the percentage of the population judged poor is reduced to 5% after taxes and transfer.

The relatively small difference between Germany and the United Kingdom on the one hand and Sweden and Norway on the other suggests a high cost at the margin for the extra degree of equalization achieved by the Scandinavian countries. This is illustrated in figure 3.1, where the extent of poverty reduction is shown with the marginal tax rate faced by the average family in these countries. Germany, the United Kingdom, and Norway have marginal tax rates in the region of 50–60% and achieve poverty reductions of the order of 70–80%. Sweden on the other hand has an exceptionally high 83% marginal tax rate with only a marginally higher performance in poverty reduction. Sweden and Norway place a small reliance on income-tested welfare benefits, thus increasing the total public expenditure required to achieve a given degree of income equalization. (Norway's marginal tax rate is lower because of the large share of petroleum taxation income in the budget.)

The situation of different types of family—elderly families, single-parent families, two-parent families, and others—helps trace the reasons for different poverty reduction results.

As regards the elderly, two points are striking. The United States record in this case is relatively close to those of Germany

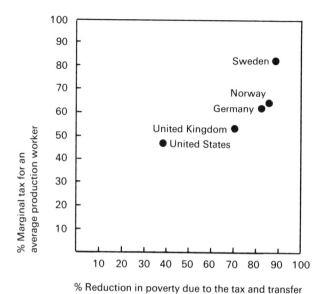

Figure 3.1
The equity-efficiency trade-off: diminution in the work incentive per unit of poverty reduction. "Reduction in poverty" is defined as displacing people from below to above the line that represents half the median income.
Sources: OECD (1986a) for the marginal rates for the combined income tax, indirect tax, and social security contribution; Smeeding et al. (1985) for the reduction in poverty.

and the United Kingdom. The US public pensions system is relatively generous. Also, the health system in the United States is relatively comprehensive for the elderly under the Medicare program. Sweden, however, goes as far as totally eliminating poverty among the elderly, with no one (or only a trivial 0.1%) remaining below the poverty line. This is due essentially to the high level of income ensured by the state pension system.

For working-age families US welfare policies reduce poverty to a much smaller degree than in Europe. In particular 52% of single-parent families remain below the poverty line after taxes

Table 3.11
Change in income distribution in the United States from 1980 to 1984 as a result of changes in taxation and transfer payment programs

Category	Reduction in benefits[a]	Reduction in taxes[a]
Less than $10,000	−7.5%	
$10,000–$20,000	−1.6%	
$20,000–$40,000	−0.4%	
$40,000–$80,000	−0.2%	
Over $80,000	−	
All households	−0.8%	
Bottom quintile		−
Second quintile		+1.4%
Third quintile		+2.8%
Fourth quintile		+4.0%
Top quintile		+5.9%
All households		+3.9%

Source: Palmer and Sawhill (1985).
a. Percentages of household income.

and transfers in the United States, whereas in Europe the remaining poor range from 29% in the United Kingdom to 9% in Sweden. A contributing factor is the absence of child allowances in the United States, alone among the OECD countries. Also important is the relatively low level and duration of unemployment benefits in the United States.

The foregoing data relate to 1979. Since then there have been some important policy changes, particularly with the Reagan administration's tax cuts and welfare program reductions.

The record of the Reagan administration's policy changes has been assessed in a study for the Urban Institute (Palmer and Sawhill 1984), and the results are summarized in table 3.11. Reductions in cash and in-kind benefits from 1980 to 1984 were substantial for the poorest category of households (7.5%), slight for middle-income households, and practically nil for the wealthiest. Income tests for income-maintenance benefits, and in some cases community work requirements ("workfare" program), have been made more restrictive (Nathan and Doolittle 1983).

On the tax side an analogous pictures is seen. The 1981 tax cuts had no impact on the poorest income quintile but was increasingly more important for higher incomes, reaching a 5.9% income gain for the top quintile of the population.

As for type of family, the elderly were largely spared from the impact of cuts in social benefits, with the whole burden therefore falling on the working-age population. This is an accentuation of main regime characteristics already noted. The United States is looking after its elderly population in a way that is relatively comparable to European countries. Tax and expenditure cuts have widened income differentials among the working-age population.

Moreover, these recent trends in tax and transfer policies add to regressive trends that have been under way since 1975, with a more unequal primary income distribution in the United States. Calculations by Harrison et al. (1986) and by Thurow (1985a) show that there has been a strong increase in income inequality in the United States, even after making various adjustments for business cycle conditions. This has reversed all the decline in income inequality observed in the 1960s and early 1970s. Fewer people are now in the medium-income bracket. From 1968 to 1984 the percentage of those whose incomes were between 75% and 125% of the median fell from 27% to 23% of the population. Both the rich and the poor became more numerous.

To summarize, the differences between the United States and Europe in the choices that their societies have made over the trade-off between work incentives and equity are wide, and since the early 1980s these differences have been widening further. To be poor and of working age and to have bad luck over one's health, for example, in the United States, is tough.

This is especially so because differences in public transfer policies between the United States and Europe are much more pronounced for those of working age than for the retired population. This sharpness of the work incentive in the United States, coupled with the comparatively light public regulation of the labor market and weak trade union power, is associated with a strong but volatile employment propensity in the economy. On all these accounts Europe is the opposite.

The challenge on the American side would seem to be to arrest and then reverse the growth of a poor and vulnerable underclass in society. Efficiency issues are involved here, as well as equity issues. Harrison et al. (1986), for example, warns that "the danger in the present context is that rising inequality—a growing gap between rich and poor—will be perceived as unbridgeable. That could undermine work incentives and thereby further erode already lagging productivity growth" (p. 8).

The challenge on the European side is to improve drastically the employment propensity of its economy while damaging as little as possible the achievements of income equity and security that have been made.

4   Return to a High-Employment Society

4.1   The Trap

The European economy has fallen into a low-employment trap. It is felt by some that this condition is not such a disagreeable one. Living standards are relatively high, and poverty is much attenuated by the welfare state. Economic growth of a modest 2–2.5% ensures slowly rising incomes. For these reasons reactions to high unemployment have not, on the whole, been violent. Indeed, some people are prepared to shrug off the unemployment problem as being practically outside the competence of economic policy. According to this view, either trade unions or some vaguely identified structural problems are responsible for creating unemployment, and social policy has to take care of the consequences. Some people look to the ending of the baby boom expansion of the labor force between 1985 and 1990 to ease the problem of youth unemployment in particular.

This view suffers from two possible weaknesses. The first is that it is unduly pessimistic in underestimating the possibilities for doing better. The second is that it may also be, paradoxically, unduly optimistic in assuming that the present, not-too-disagreeable low-employment society is sustainable.

On the first point it can hardly be denied that the low-employment society in Europe represents a massive under-performance of European society in relation to its human potential. Any argument that shows how this potential can be more fully realized without imposing unacceptable political or social conditions should be considered with favor. This is the argument that follows in section 4.2.

On the second point the problem of sustainability is most concretely illustrated by the pensions issue. As we showed in chapter 3, with the present policies the rising burden of pension payments, from the 1990s leading well into the next century, means that a simple extrapolation of present trends is unsustainable. Either pensions will have to be drastically cut, implying serious issues of income distribution between the generations, or social security taxes will have to be further increased by a substantial margin. A tax increase would risk opening a new round of stagflationary impulses; new labor taxes depress employment trends and so further weaken the tax base, thus calling for further tax increases. The pension issue draws attention in a particularly sharp way to the broader question of whether Europe's remarkable social achievements of the postwar period can be sustained on present macroeconomic and employment trends. As Albert (1983) has described, the whole array of social benefits is at stake, be it pensions, health care, family benefits, or other programs. The only way to sustain a high level of social benefits like those just mentioned is to increase the employment base of the economy. A high-employment society can afford high standards of social security; a low-employment society cannot.

Before turning to prescriptions, let us recapitulate the origins and nature of the low-employment trap. Excellent analyses have been set out in detail; see, for example, Bruno and Sachs (1985) for both theory and empirical assessments.

When the first oil shock arrived in 1973, Western Europe had been growing quickly for two decades. Unemployment was 2.5% of the labor force; that is, there was full employment. Real incomes were accelerating; employment protection laws were being made more demanding; welfare benefits were being generalized and upgraded. The stagflationary shocks of the first and then, in 1979–1980, the second oil crisis saw in Europe only slow adjustments of the wage system to the needs of the situation, that is, lower nominal settlements to speed disinflation and lower real settlements to avoid a serious erosion of profits and investment. Recession brought large increases in public expenditure on unemployment benefits and other transfer payments. Because of the apparently structural rather than benign cyclical origin of the recession, governments braked the rise in budget deficits, especially with increases in social security contributions. Employment trends became further depressed because of the weak demand situation, raising wage and social security costs and perceptions of increased indirect labor costs in the form of employment protection laws. Palliatives such as expanded programs of invalidity and early retirement pensions may have dampened the growth of officially registered unemployment during the first shock, but it contributed further to rising social security taxes and so further discouraged employment. Thus Europe drifted into a vicious circle of depressed employment and rising tax burdens. Tough public-expenditure-cutting programs sought to limit the rise of taxation or budget deficits, but by the mid-1980s this had gone no further than to stabilize the GDP ratios of these public finance aggregates, given the rising burden of social expenditure on the unemployed.

The outcome for the evolution of public expenditures on social programs is shown in table 4.1. From 1970 to 1983 there was in the European Community a very large 10% of GDP increase in public expenditure on these items; to a large extent this was matched by increases in social security contributions, with the budget deficit also taking part of the strain. One-quarter of this increase in social expenditure was directly spent on unemployment benefits. Another 10% of the increase was spent on invalidity and disability pensions, of which a consider-

Table 4.1
Breakdown of the increase in social benefits in eight European Community countries between 1970 and 1983[a]

Expenditure	1970 (% of GDP)	1983 (% of GDP)	Increase
Health care, sickness	5.0	6.7	1.7
Invalidity, work injury	2.1	2.9	.8
Pensions	7.9	11.1	3.1
Family benefits	2.3	2.6	0.2
Unemployment	0.3	2.5	2.3
Other	0.2	0.4	0.2
Total	18.0	27.0	9.0

Source: See appendix A, table A.25.
a. Average of eight countries. The table excludes Italy, whose total public expenditure over the period 1970–1983 rose by 23% of GDP, no doubt raising the European Community average increase in social expenditures of 9% for the countries covered to 10% or slightly more.

able share reflected the expansion of programs to remove the long-term unemployed from the labor force. The largest share in the increase, about one-third, was spent on pensions, of which a significant share was due to reductions in the retirement age and special schemes for early retirement. Thus in total there was an increase in the share of GDP of perhaps $7\frac{1}{2}\%$ transferred in favor of the inactive population: the unemployed and the pensioned. The increased GDP share of these benefits is, of course, by definition additional to the rise in the level of such benefits in line with the economic growth.

By comparison, other main social benefits showed smaller, if any, increases. Family benefits were held almost unchanged as a share of GDP, despite the fact that this heading includes some programs of means-tested family income maintenance for which there were more clients. Health care contributed about 20% to the total rise of social benefits. In this sector there is a rise in the relative prices of services as well as a high income elasticity of demand.

The level of social security taxes in Western Europe has thus risen to very high levels (see table 4.2), averaging 43% of the wage tax base for the four largest countries, as against about 20% in both the United States and Japan. Of this, employers typically pay a 30% tax in Western Europe (average of the same four countries), whereas they pay only 11–12% in the United States and Japan. The figures for Europe are tax rates subject in some cases (in Germany and the United Kingdom but not France or Italy) to ceiling income levels, which means that average tax rates can be lower. However, this nonproportionality in the tax rate acts as a relative disincentive to employing low-income personnel, which is hardly a helpful feature at the present time.

In 1985 European employers, surveyed by the Commission of the European Communities (1986a), rated the level of social security costs and the problems of rigid employment protection laws highly as a reason why they were not able to employ more people. Although the low level of demand was rated as the most important reason, the level of wage costs and other reasons, such as technological advances and shortages of skilled applicants, were rated as less important than social security costs and employment protection laws.

4.2   Springing the Trap

Looking ahead to where one might like the European economy to be in five to ten years' time, especially in the employment domain, necessitates some degree of arbitrariness. Some license is required to set out numbers for illustrative purposes. A return to a 5% unemployment rate would be considered rather satisfactory after the last ten years' experience. But a higher labor force participation rate should be associated with this for two reasons. There are effectively unemployed people beyond the official register: discouraged workers and those on early pensions of various kinds. In addition, the demographic and pension prob-

Table 4.2
Social security contributions in 1983

Country	Employer contribution (%)	Employee contribution (%)	Total
United States	12.0	6.7	18.7
Japan	11.0	10.1	21.1
France	46.5	13.9	60.4
Germany	18.8	17.3	36.1
Italy	45.6	8.6	54.2
United Kingdom	10.5	9.0	19.5
Total four countries above[a]	30.4	12.2	42.6
Belgium	38.8	10.8	49.6
The Netherlands	24.5	38.8	63.2
Denmark	–	4.5	4.5
Finland	5.5	2.7	8.2
Norway	16.2	10.1	26.3
Sweden	30.5	–	30.5
Switzerland	10.2	10.2	20.2
Austria	22.2	15.6	37.6
Ireland	11.6	8.5	20.1
Spain	31.8	5.5	37.3
Portugal	21.5	11.5	32.0

Source: OECD (1986a).
a. Unweighted average.

Table 4.3
Summary of a high-employment society in the European Community

Quantity	Low-employment society (1986)	High-employment society in seven or so years' time	Change
Unemployment			
millions	13	6	−7
% labor force	10.5	4.5	−6.0
Employment			
millions	108	126	+18
Labor force			
millions	121	132	+11
% of population	65.9	71.0	+5.9

lem ahead points to the need to put the economy onto a trend of rising participation rates among those who are fit enough physically to work full- or part-time. It is supposed therefore that the participation rate for those aged 15 to 64 in the European Community might rise from $65\frac{1}{2}$% in 1986 to 71% some seven years later. Both the United States and Japan are currently at the 73% level, and Sweden is at 81%.

The high-employment society in the European Community of some years ahead is summarized in table 4.3 (this is the result of a quantified simulation explained in the next pages and set out in detail in appendix B). The achievement of 18 million extra jobs over seven years would require a growth of employment of a little over 2% a year. Associated with an annual productivity growth of nearly 2%, this would imply a sustained growth of GDP of 3–4% per annum.

The question is now whether the adjustments that have been recommended in earlier chapters for the European model of social security systems and pay determination could help achieve objectives of this order of magnitude. Could a medium-term program, which combined social security and wage adjustments together with supporting macroeconomic policies, add up to the core of a strategy for returning to a high-employment society?

To answer this question, we adopt a number of formal hypotheses for adjustments to social security taxes and benefits, macroeconomic policy variables (budgetary, monetary, exchange rate), and some temporary change in trend in wage incomes. The effects of the program are then simulated with the aid of a macroeconometric model of the European economy. This simulation is set out in detail in appendix B, together with a summary of the theoretical characteristics of the model [full details of which are published in Dramais (1986)]. The simulation, although a simplified account of reality, nonetheless shows that the program could form the basis of a strategy for returning to a high-employment society.

The strategy is centered around the cuts in social security costs that could be achieved in the course of returning to high employment levels. Armed with estimates of these savings, obtained directly through less expenditure on both unemployment benefits and early retirement pensions and indirectly through other budgetary dividends from faster growth, the authorities should be able to decide on a medium-term program of social security tax cuts of corresponding magnitude. At the same time, eligibility criteria for early retirement benefits would be changed for new beneficiaries in the manner earlier envisaged (section 3.3). Thus the supply as well as the demand for labor would be increased. Employment would be increased, first, as a result of lower social security taxes and therefore labor costs and, second, as the rate of macroeconomic growth increased. Macroeconomic policy would be supportive in the sense that it would aim to keep the growth of aggregate nominal demand in the economy on a steady growth trajectory. With lower labor costs there would also be reductions in price inflation, and therefore a steady macroeconomic growth strategy in the sense just mentioned would authorize budgetary and monetary policy actions to sustain aggregate demand.

Some of the key magnitudes are as follows. With the reduction of unemployment to about 5%, there would be a direct saving to the budget of about $1\frac{1}{4}$% of GDP through lower unemployment benefits. The phasing out of early retirement pensions and invalidity benefits (for those without serious medical impairment) could possibly save a further 2% of GDP. The additional 18 million employed persons would, at normal social security tax rates, provide the budget with increased revenues to the extent of $1\frac{1}{4}$% of GDP; however, because it is envisaged that there would be extensive social security subsidies for older workers and for those who had earlier been long-term unemployed, this saving might be reduced to 1% of GDP. Total savings to the budget might thus amount to $4\frac{1}{2}$% of GDP. Social security tax cuts of an equivalent amount over a five-year period are made accordingly (1% of GDP in each of four years, and $\frac{1}{2}$% of GDP in the fifth).

The cuts in social security taxes would represent a reduction by about one-third of the total burden of these taxes. In 1983 in the European Community such taxes amounted to 15% of GDP, which in turn represented 28% of the tax base represented by wage and salary incomes; the average social security tax rates, ignoring the effect of ceilings, were 42%. If we assume that tax reductions of the magnitude indicated are split 3 to 1 between employers and employees, respectively (that is, proportionately in relation to present rates), then the labour costs would be reduced 7% and employees' take home pay increased by 3%. A labor cost reduction of this magnitude could on its own be expected to lead after three to five years to a similar 7% expansion of employment. [An elasticity of employment to labor costs, after a medium-run time lag, of about unity is reflected in the working of the model and is also supported by other econometric studies; see Layard et al. (1985)]. This accounts for almost half of the employment growth envisaged for the high-employment society. The remaining extra jobs would be accounted for by the other favorable factors: higher economic growth in the first place, plus employment subsidies (reduced social security tax for marginal workers), higher real wage flexibility associated with profit-sharing, lower fixed labor costs associated with less stringent employment protection laws, and greater intersectoral wage flexibility associated with minimum wage reforms.

As regards macroeconomic policy, the disinflationary impact of the social security tax cuts authorizes, according to the principles already explained, a temporary expansion of public investment during the first three years (cumulating to $1\frac{1}{2}\%$ of GDP) before being phased out in the subsequent three years. Monetary expansion is slightly increased, and the exchange rate depreciates by a small margin. A policy of wage moderation is implemented for the first two years of the program, as a result of which nominal wages increase 2% less than otherwise would have been the case in each year. The government's budget deficit is increased by a moderate amount during the first two years, thereafter declining until it reaches in the seventh year the level originally projected in the absence of the strategy.

The overall results are that economic growth is raised to a little over 4% for a few years before settling down to a $3\frac{1}{2}\%$ sustainable medium-term trend. Employment growth averages 2.1% over a seven-year period, and the unemployment rate reaches the 5% target in the course of the seventh year. The labor force participation rate reaches 71%. The increase in total employment by 18 million is also achieved in the seventh year.

The viability of this macroeconomic arithmetic hangs on (1) whether sufficient influences restraining wage settlements can be assembled to allow the high-employment society to be achieved without provoking an inflationary wage explosion and (2) whether these influences amount to a change in social policies that can command a broad support in public and political opinion. Will the revised European model hold? Will it be acceptable?

As regards the wage trend, a special moderation would be called for in the first two years as part of a social compact whose principal objective was a permanent return to high employment levels. Base wages would increase little in real terms for a few years. However, real income gains would be ensured by cuts in social security taxes (employee's part) and by profit-linked increases in bonus payments where the situation warrants this. Labor supply would also be augmented by changes in early retirement and related policies. The demand for labor would in part be guided toward these new sources of labor supply as a result of reduced social security levies for recruitment from among the long-term unemployed, young, and relatively elderly working population. Minimum wage policies would be more flexible. Moderation of rigid hiring and firing rules would also temper wage claims. (The effect of these last measures have not been built into the model simulation.)

As regards political acceptability, it should be emphasized that fundamental social security goals are being maintained and indeed protected from the threats of economic unsustainability. Thus the universal availability of public health care, pensions, family benefits, and means-tested income maintenance would be kept. Employment protection legislation would also be retained, providing a legal support for the concept of fair dismissal and regulated procedures for collective dismissals. Social security policies for those who could work but presently do not and labor market policies on hiring and firing would be reformed so as to attentuate features that were most harmful to employment. [For other contributions along these lines, see Sachs and Wyplosz (1986).]

A further important issue concerns the time sequence of the various micro- and macroeconomic policy moves implied in this scheme. Timing would be vital to achieve a strong, credible impulse in the beginning so that expectations would change and medium-term employment and investment plans would begin to be influenced early on. The microeconomic policy measures—reforms of employment protection law, changes of early retirement and disability pension policies, changes in minimum wage and incomes policies, employment subsidies for the selected groups—should be as front-loaded as possible. The cuts in social security taxes should be a leading element but far from wholly front-loaded. Budget deficits would end the period at the same level as otherwise, and so the social security tax cuts would be self-financing when combined with the other microeconomic policy moves. In this way supply and demand factors could interact in a dynamic manner.

As regards pensions policy, a point of clarification and emphasis is warranted. It was suggested earlier that present pension policies pose a threat to the sustainability of present economic trends in Europe. It was also argued that policies to increase labor force participation are desirable to improve the present economic situation. Are the same reforms to increase labor force participation being counted twice? No, but similar measures would be seen in two successive phases. In the first period, in the next five years or so, labor force participation should be increased with a phasing-out of early retirement subsidies and the promotion of employment of older workers. This would be part of the process of returning to a high-employment society relatively soon. In the second phase there would then remain the pension policy problem of the turn of the century and beyond. For this it is envisaged that the average retirement age would be raised gradually over several decades, accompanied by actuarially neutral arrangements to permit a wider choice of retirement age. The first phase would also prepare the way for the second phase, with enterprises and government policies becoming adapted to securing a long-term trend of a gradually aging labor force.

4.3 Concluding Remarks

No suggestions for a European socioeconomic model could be considered eligible for consideration if they did not contain a dynamic element designed to lift the European economy out of its present low-employment condition. Therefore a few pages have been devoted to a sketch of the dynamic process intended to accompany the suggestions set out in the preceding sections. However, our main purpose has not been to work out an economic policy program but rather to reflect on long-run model characteristics of the European economy, compared to those of the United States and Japan.

The recommended European model is based, hardly surprisingly, on the existing one. However, the recommended model adapts the existing one, borrowing some attractive features from the United States and Japan but retaining its own specific cocktail.

In the realm of wage determination the recommended model would see some moves in Europe in the direction of Japanese profit-sharing to enhance real wage flexibility and also some move in the direction of United States and Japanese minimum wage policies that are nationally regulated but in a less constraining way than in much of Europe. Wage cuts, however, are not advocated as part of a strategy to return to high employment. Others cuts in labor costs are sought—in social security taxes and some employment protection provisions as indicated in what follows.

As regards employment protection regulations, the totally nonregulated United States model is not favored, and a gradual evolution diluting the free hiring and firing tradition in that country may be expected. In much of Europe, however, excessively onerous employment protection law is a hindrance to achieving higher employment levels, and Japan again has some interesting policies for mixing a strong preference for employment security with features giving labor market flexibility.

In the domain of core social policies—health care, education, and old-age pensions—the main regime characteristics in Europe are not fundamentally faulted. In health care and public schooling the United States has particularly serious problems to overcome. In Europe the financing of higher education could possibly be aided with more recourse to student loans, as in the United States. As regards public old-age pensions, important policy changes will be required in Europe as in Japan to avoid grave financial imbalances in the next century. In this respect the United States policy of announcing well in advance gradual increases in the normal retirement age for the early decades of the twenty-first century deserves serious consideration in Europe; this would reverse policy trends that have been more in evidence in recent years in several European countries.

As regards income-maintenance policies for those of working age, Europe has slipped into a badly faulted situation. Europe's preference for a much more equal income distribution than the United States can certainly be justified. The equity-efficiency trade-off can be different in different societies, and the traditions in many European countries in favor of corporatist cooperation in economic and social policies have helped achieve remarkable combinations of high productivity and equity. The present situation, however, sees most countries in Europe paying extremely large sums from public budgets to people who could work but do not. The fiscal burden of this declining labor force participation and high unemployment either threatens the funding of other vital public services or dampens the employment propensity of the economy in a vicious circle of depressing influences. Coupled with a growing problem of pension funding, this adds up to a serious threat to the existing achievements of the socioeconomic model, hence the importance of measures to reverse the declining labor force participation rate and to reduce registered unemployment. In terms of the model of the social security system this would imply only marginal changes in unemployment benefit systems (for example, the duration of benefits and administrative rules on what work should be accepted), but it would imply bigger changes in reversing recent tendencies to expand programs of different kinds for permanently pensioning people who could contribute normally to the labor force. Such changes would need to be accompanied by macroeconomic and microeconomic employment stimulation policies of a kind outlined in the preceding section. Large cuts in social security taxes would be critical to the chances of setting in motion a dynamic process that would return Europe to a high-employment society.

Appendix A

Social Security Systems in the Industrialized Countries

Table A.1
Unemployment benefits in 1985

Country	Unemployment benefit
United States	50% of earnings (approx.) for 26–34 weeks plus up to 13 weeks in selected regions
Japan	60–80% of earnings for 3–12 months, depending on age and other criteria
France	Fr40/day plus 42% of earnings for $1-2\frac{1}{2}$ years; also special allowance, 3 years
Germany	68% of earnings for up to 1 year, then 58% indefinitely
Italy	L500/day for 180 days; special layoff benefit for industry of 80% of earnings for 3–12 months (sometimes longer)
United Kingdom	£28.5/week for 52 weeks
Belgium	60% of earnings; 40%, second year; then 50% of minimum wage indefinitely
The Netherlands	70% of earnings (maximum of F262 daily) for 26 weeks, then 70% with means test up to 2 years
Denmark	90% of earnings (maximum of Kr335 daily) for up to $2\frac{1}{2}$ years
Norway	73% of earnings (maximum of Kr310 daily) for up to 40 weeks
Finland	Maximum of 75% of earnings or M70/day for up to 450 days in 3 years
Sweden	Kr80–300/day for 1 year
Switzerland	75–80% of earnings for 150 days
Austria	30–60% of earnings, varying inversely with wage, for up to 30 weeks
Ireland	£39.5/week plus 20–40% of earnings, varying inversely with wage (85% max.) for up to 390 days
Spain	80% of earnings for 180 days; 70% to 12th month; 60% to 18th month
Greece	40–50% of earnings, depending on income, for 50–125 days
Portugal	70% of minimum wage for 180 days (sometimes longer)

Source: United States Department of Health and Human Services (1985).

Table A.2
Sickness and maternity benefits in 1985[a]

Country	Benefit
United States	No federal program; 6 states provide 5–66% of earnings, 44 states none
Japan	60% of earnings, M
France	50% of earnings for 30 days, 66% thereafter if 3 or more children; M +
Germany	100% of earnings for 6 weeks, up to 80% thereafter; M
Italy	50% of earnings for 20 days, 66% thereafter; M +
United Kingdom	52–84% of earnings for up to 6 months, with ceilings; M
Belgium	60% of earnings for 1 year, with ceiling; M
The Netherlands	70% of earnings for 1 year, with ceiling; M +
Denmark	90% of earnings for unlimited period, with ceiling; M
Norway	100% of earnings for 1 year; M
Finland	80% of earnings for up to 300 days; M
Sweden	90% of earnings, with ceiling; M
Switzerland	Minimum Fr2/day, higher according to fund, for up to 720 days; M
Austria	100% of earnings for 4–12 weeks, thereafter 75% maximum for 28 weeks; M
Spain	60% of earnings for up to 21 days, thereafter 75% up to 12–18 months; M +
Greece	50% of earnings (plus 100% for each dependent) for up to 180 days, with ceiling; M
Portugal	60% of earnings for up to 3 years; M +

Source: United States Department of Health and Human Services (1985).
a. The table describes sickness benefits. "M" signifies maternity benefits of the same level as sickness benefits, with particular time limits. "M +" signifies a higher level of maternity benefits.

Table A.3
Old-age pension benefits (public) in 1985

Country	Pension benefit
United States	$122–709/month
Japan	¥2050/month plus 1% of revalued lifetime earnings × years of coverage
France	50% of average revalued earnings of last 10 years
Germany	1.5% of average earnings of last 3 years × years of coverage
Italy	2% of average revalued earnings of last 5 years × years of coverage
United Kingdom	£35.8/week plus 1.25% of covered earnings × years of coverage from 1978
Belgium	60% of average lifetime revalued earnings
The Netherlands	F1161/month
Denmark	Kr2956/month
Norway	Kr24,200/year plus 45% difference between covered earnings and a base amount.
Finland	M307/month
Sweden	Kr1744/month plus 60% difference between covered earnings and a base amount
Switzerland	Fr552/month plus 1.67% average annual revalued earnings
Austria	1.9% of average earnings of last 5 years × years of coverage, 79.5% maximum.
Ireland	£51.4/week
Spain	50% of highest earnings in 2 of last 7 years plus 2% of years of average earnings between 11 and 35 years
Greece	30–70% of last 2 years earnings plus 1–2.5% for each 300 days of contribution beyond 3000 days
Portugal	2.2% × annual average earnings of highest 5 of last 10 years; 30% minimum, 70% maximum

Source: United States Department of Health and Human Services (1985).

Table A.4
Invalidity and disability benefits in 1985[a]

Country	Invalidity benefits	Disability benefits
United States	similar to pension	66% of earnings in most states
Japan	as pension	maximum of 86% of earnings
France	as pension	maximum of 100% of earnings
Germany	as pension	maximum of 66% of earnings plus 10% for each dependent child
Italy	as pension	maximum of 100% of earnings plus 5% for each dependent child
United Kingdom	similar to pension	maximum of £56.4/week
Belgium	43.5% of earnings, 66% with dependents	maximum of 100% of earnings
The Netherlands	70% of earnings	maximum of 70% of earnings
Denmark	as pension plus supplements	maximum of 75% of earnings
Norway	as pension	maximum of 100% of earnings
Finland	as pension	85% of earnings plus 40% supplements for total disability
Sweden	similar to pension	maximum of 100% of earnings
Switzerland	as pension	maximum of 80% of earnings
Austria	as pension	maximum of 66% of earnings plus 10% for each dependent child
Ireland	£45.3/week	£54.4/week plus 20–40% prior income
Spain	maximum of 100% of earnings	maximum of 100% of earnings
Greece	as pension	same as invalidity but minimum of 60% of earnings
Portugal	as pension	maximum of 50–66% of earnings

Source: United States Department of Health and Human Services (1985).
a. Invalidity benefits are due to illness; disability benefits are those due to work injury.

Table A.5
Family and income-maintenance benefits in 1985[a]

Country	Child benefits for family with 3 children, amount per month[b]	Other programs
United States	–	means-tested benefits for single parent households and food stamps
Japan	¥5000 ($31)	supplement for low-income families
France	Fr1449 ($207)	means-tested family supplement, guaranteed minimum family income
Germany	DM260 ($118)	means-tested unemployment assistance of indefinite duration
Italy	L59,280 ($39)	means-tested family supplement
United Kingdom	£20.6 ($32)	means-tested family supplement
Belgium	Fr11,479 ($255)	guaranteed minimum family income
The Netherlands	F49 ($21)[c]	unemployment assistance for 2 years
Denmark	Kr573 ($70)	means-tested youth allowance
Finland	M1113 ($218)	unemployment assistance of long duration
Sweden	Kr1400 ($197)	means-tested social assistance
Switzerland	Fr250 ($139)	means-tested benefit of aged
Austria	S3000 ($194)	unemployment assistance of long duration
Ireland	£36.1 ($50)	unemployment assistance of long duration
Spain	Pta750 ($5)	temporary assistance for needy
Greece	Dr5850 ($42)	–
Portugal	$1800 ($12)	–

Source: United States Department of Health and Human Services (1985).
a. The table omits categorical benefits that are sometimes of importance, such as housing help and school meals.
b. Values in parentheses indicate equivalent amounts in June 1986 US dollars.
c. Amount for one child. Amount rises to F189 ($81) for eight children.

Table A.6
Health care benefits (public) in 1985

Country	Health care benefits
United States	no comprehensive system; aged and poor get 80% refund on doctors, drugs, and laboratory work and 90 days free hospitalization
Japan	comprehensive coverage; patients pay 30% under national health service
France	comprehensive coverage; refunds 75–100% of charges
Germany	comprehensive coverage; some charges for drugs and dentistry
Italy	comprehensive coverage; patient pays 50% of charges for dentistry
United Kingdom	comprehensive coverage except charges for dentistry (but free for children, poor)
Belgium	comprehensive coverage; refunds 75–100% of charges
The Netherlands	comprehensive coverage; some dental and other charges
Denmark	comprehensive coverage; patient pays 25% of charges for drugs, some dental charges
Norway	comprehensive coverage; refunds 51–100% for doctor's bills, charges for drugs
Finland	comprehensive coverage; refunds 60% for doctors, 75% for laboratory costs, 50% for drugs; hospitals free
Sweden	comprehensive coverage; patient pays 20% for doctors, 50% for drugs, 60% for dentistry (except children free); hospitals free
Switzerland	comprehensive coverage; patient pays 10% for drugs
Austria	comprehensive coverage; patient pays charges for drugs, 20% dental charges
Ireland	comprehensive; some charges
Spain	comprehensive coverage; patient pays 40% for drugs
Greece	comprehensive coverage; patient pays 20–25% of charges; hospitals free
Portugal	comprehensive coverage; some cost-sharing

Source: United States Department of Health and Human Services (1985).

Table A.7
Main features of various benefits for the United States, 1961–1985

Year	Old-age pension[a]	Invalidity[b]	Disability[c]	Sickness[d]	Unemployment[e]	Health care
1961	$40–127	as pension	$60–66\frac{2}{3}\%$	—	50%	—
1964	$40–127	"	"	—	"	—
1967	$40–168	"	"	—	"	no universal system; since 1967 for those over 65 years of age, 90 days free hopitalization and 80% of doctor's laboratory fees (Medicare); poor people get free medical treatment (Medicaid).
1969	$55–218	"	"	—	"	"
1971	$64–250	"	"	—	"	"
1973	$85–266	"	"	—	"	"
1975	$94–316	"	"	—	"	"
1977	$108–413	"	$66\frac{2}{3}\%$	—	"	"
1979	$122–514	"	"	—	"	"
1981	$122–677	"	"	—	"	"
1983	$122–709	"	"	—	"	"
1985	$0–717	$0–909	"	—	"	"

Source: United States Department of Health and Human Services, *Social Security Programs throughout the World* (various issues).
a. Minimum and maximum per month; 50% more for dependent spouse or child.
b. Same as old-age pension, except for maximum level in recent years.
c. $66\frac{2}{3}\%$ of prior earnings in most states for total disablement from work injury.
d. No federal scheme; no state scheme in 45 states. New York pays 50% of earnings.
e. About 50%, varying a little by state, payable for 26–34 weeks with some extensions.

Table A.8
Main features of various benefits for Japan, 1961–1985

Year	Old-age pension[a]	Disability[b]	Sickness[c]	Unemployment[d]	Health care[e]
1961	¥167 + 0.6%	$66\frac{2}{3}$%	60%	60%	comprehensive, patient pays 30%
1964	"	"	"	"	"
1967	¥250 + 1%	60%	"	"	"
1969	"	"	"	"	"
1971	¥400 + 1%	"	"	62–72%	"
1973	¥460 + 1%	"	"	60%	"
1975	¥1000 + 1%	"	"	60–80%	"
1977	¥1650 + 1%	"	"	"	"
1979	¥2050 + 1%	"	"	"	"
1981	"	"	"	"	"
1983	"	"	"	"	"
1985	"	"	"	"	"

Source: See table A.7.

a. Yen per month plus percentage of revalued average lifetime earnings × years of service; plus ¥15,000 per month for spouse. Invalidity benefits same as pension.

b. For totally disabled through work injury.

c. Percent of last 3 months' earnings.

d. Benefits payable for 90–300 days in 1 year.

e. National health service benefits. This provides for those not covered by compulsory employee's schemes, which require different patient charges. Patients were charged 50% in 1961, this being reduced to 30% from 1964 onward.

Table A.9
Main features of various benefits for France, 1961–1985

Year	Old-age pension[a]	Invalidity[b]	Disability[c]	Sickness[d]	Unemployment	Health care
1961	20% (40%)	50%	100%	$50-66\frac{2}{3}$%	Fr4.2[e]	comprehensive, refunds 75–100%
1964	"	"	"	"	"	"
1967	"	"	"	"	Fr6.2[e]	"
1969	"	"	"	"	40%	"
1971	"	"	"	"	35–40%[f]	"
1973	22.6% (45%)	"	"	"	"	"
1975	25% (50%)	"	"	"	"	"
1977	"	"	"	"	25–40%[f]	"
1979	25% (50%)	"	"	"	42% + Fr20[g]	"
1981	25% (50%)	"	"	"	42% + Fr22[g]	"
1983	50%	"	"	"	42% + Fr25[g]	"
1985	50%	"	"	—	42% + Fr40[g]	"

Source: See table A.7.

a. Percentage of average earnings of highest 10 years, revalued for wage changes; plus spouse's supplement. Number in parentheses indicates arduous work/dependent.

b. Percentage of highest paid 10 years if totally disabled.

c. Percentage of average earnings during last 10 months if totally disabled through work injury.

d. Rising to $66\frac{2}{3}$% after 30 days if 3 or more children.

e. Per day.

f. Falling to lower amount after 3 months, maximum 1 year.

g. Fixed sum per day plus percentage of earnings for up to $2\frac{1}{2}$ years. Those laid off for economic reasons entitled to higher benefits of 50–75% of earnings during first year, with a minimum of 90% of the minimum wage (since 1983).

Table A.10
Main features of various benefits for Germany, 1961–1985

Year	Old-age pension[a]	Disability[b]	Sickness	Unemployment[d]	Health care
1961	1.5%	60$\frac{2}{3}$%	75–90%[c]	40–90%	comprehensive, some charges for prescriptions and dentures
1964	"	"	75–100%[c]	"	"
1967	"	"	"	"	"
1969	"	"	"	62.5%	"
1971	"	"	"	"	"
1973	"	"	"	"	"
1975	"	"	80–100%	68%	"
1977	"	"	"	"	"
1979	"	"	"	"	"
1981	"	"	"	41–69%	"
1983	"	"	"	"	"
1985	"	"	"	68%	"

Source: See table A.7.

a. Percentage of last 3 years' average earnings × years of coverage. Invalidity benefits same as pension.

b. Percentage of last year's earnings for totally disabled through work injury.

c. Higher percentage for first 6 weeks, lower percentage thereafter, plus 4% for spouse, 3% for each child.

d. Percentage declining inversely with income; payable for up to 1 year, followed by indefinite "unemployment assistance," currently 58% (income tested).

Table A.11
Main features of various benefits for Italy, 1961–1985

Year	Old-age pension[a]	Disability[b]	Sickness[c]	Unemployment[d]	Health care
1961	L6500/80% max.	100%	50%	L300/66$\frac{2}{3}$%	comprehensive, patient pays 50% of dental costs
1964	L1200/80% max.	"	50–66$\frac{2}{3}$%	"	"
1967	L15000/80% max.	"	"	L400/66$\frac{2}{3}$%	"
1969	1.85%/80% max.	"	"	"	"
1971	"	"	"	"	"
1973	"	"	"	"	"
1975	"	"	"	L800/66$\frac{2}{3}$%	"
1977	2%/80% max.	"	"	L800/80%	"
1979	"	"	"	"	comprehensive
1981	"	"	"	"	"
1983	"	"	"	"	"
1985	"	"	"	"	"

Source: See table A.7.

a. For earlier years the minimum is the amount of lire per month; the maximum is 80% of average earnings. For later years, benefit is a percentage of average earnings of last 5 years, revalued, × years of coverage, subject to 80% maximum. Invalidity benefits same as pension.

b. For totally disabled through work injury.

c. Higher percentage after 20 days.

d. Fixed number of lire per day for up to 180 days in the general regime; for industrial workers 66$\frac{2}{3}$% or later 80% of earnings is paid to laid-off workers (by the Cassa Integrazione Guadenzi).

Table A.12
Main features of various benefits for the United Kingdom, 1961–1985

Year	Old-age pension[a]	Invalidity[b]	Disability[c]	Sickness[d]	Unemployment	Health care
1961	£2.875 + graduated element	as pension	£4.875	as unemployment	£2.875[e]	comprehensive, patient pays some dental and prescription charges
1964	£3.375 + graduated element	"	£5.75	"	£3.35[e]	"
1967	£4 + graduated element	"	£6.75	"	£4[f]	"
1969	£5 + graduated element	"	£8.4	"	£5[f]	"
1971	£5 + graduated element	"	£8.4	"	£5[f]	"
1973	£6.75 + graduated element	"	£11.20	"	£6.75[f]	"
1975	£11.6 + graduated element	"	£19	"	£9.8[f]	"

Table A.12 (continued)

Year	Old-age pension[a]	Invalidity[b]	Disability[c]	Sickness[d]	Unemployment	Health care
1977	£15.3 + graduated element	"	£25	"	£12.9[f]	"
1979	£19.5 + 1.25%	"	£35.9	"	£15.75[f]	"
1981	£27.15 + 1.25%	"	£44.3	"	£20.65[f]	"
1983	£32.85 + 1.25%	£31.45 +	£53.6	"	£25[g]	"
1985	£35.8 + 1.25%	£34.25 +	£56.4	£27.25 +	£28.45[g]	"

Source: See table A.7.

a. Amount in pounds per week plus 60% more for spouse; graduated element = £0.025 per £7.5 of contributions, or, later 1.25% of earnings × years of coverage.

b. Basic amount plus supplement according to age at incapacity.

c. Amount in pounds per week for totally disabled through work injury.

d. From 1985 basic amount for low incomes, graduated rises for higher incomes.

e. Amount in pounds per week plus 60% for spouse and more for children, plus graduated element of 33% of income range (in excess of low wage), maximum 85% of earnings.

f. Same as note e, except maximum amount of graduated element is 80%.

g. Same as note e, except graduated element abolished.

Table A.13
Main features of various benefits for Belgium, 1961–1985

Year	Old-age pension[a]	Invalidity[b]	Disability[c]	Sickness[d]	Unemployment[e]	Health care
1961	60/75%	60%, max. Fr138	100%	60%, max. Fr138	Fr109, $66\frac{2}{3}\%$	Comprehensive, refund 75%, except 100% for serious treatment
1964	"	60%, max. Fr420	"	"	Fr124, $66\frac{2}{3}\%$	"
1967	"	40/60%	"	"	Fr130, $66\frac{2}{3}\%$	"
1969	"	"	"	60%, max. Fr245	Fr198, $66\frac{2}{3}\%$	"
1971	"	"	"	60%, max. Fr264	Fr256, $66\frac{2}{3}\%$	"
1973	"	"	"	60%, max. Fr401	60%	"
1975	"	$43\frac{1}{2}$/65%	"	60%, max. Fr910	"	"
1977	"	"	"	60%, max. Fr1088	"	"
1979	"	"	"	60%, max. Fr1201	"	"
1981	"	"	"	60%, max. Fr1352	"	"
1983	"	"	"	60%, max. Fr1585	"	"
1985	"	"	"	60%, max. Fr1715	"	"

Source: See table A.7.

a. Percentage of average lifetime earnings, revalued; 60% single, 75% with spouse.

b. Single person, lower percentage; with spouse, higher percentage. Amounts in francs per day.

c. Percentage of earnings for totally disabled through work injury.

d. Percentage of earnings in francs per day.

e. Amount in francs per day for person with dependent, duration indefinite.

Table A.14
Main features of various benefits for the Netherlands, 1961–1985

Year	Old-age pension[a]	Invalidity[b]	Disability	Sickness	Unemployment[c]	Health care
1961	F95	—	70%	80%	70%	comprehensive, patient pays some dental fees, some other cost-sharing
1964	F147	F327	"	"	"	"
1967	F241	80%, max. F624	80%	"	80%	"
1969	F309	80%, max. F644	"	"	"	"
1971	F380	"	"	"	"	"
1973	F492	"	"	80%, max. F125	"	"
1975	F642	80%, max. F164	80%, max. F164	80%, max. F164	80%, max. F164	"
1977	F804	"	"	"	F198	"
1979	F920	"	"	"	F225	"
1981	F1099	"	"	"	F243	"
1983	F1155	"	"	"	F262	"
1985	F1161	70%, max. F262	70%, max. F262	70%, max. F262	70%, max. F262	"

Source: See table A.7.
a. Amounts in gulden per month for single person, increased about 42% with spouse.
b. 80% of earnings if over 80% disabled, in gulden per month.
c. Before 1964, 70% for single person, 80% with spouse; from 1964, generally 80%. Amounts in gulden per day.

Table A.15
Main features of various benefits for Denmark, 1961–1985

Year	Old-age pension[a]	Disability[b]	Sickness[c]	Unemployment[d]	Health care
1961	Kr300	$66\frac{2}{3}$%	80%, Kr4–6	80% max., Kr10–13	Comprehensive, patient pays 25% prescriptions, some dental fees
1964	Kr400	"	80%, Kr16	80% max., Kr13–19	"
1967	Kr517	"	80%, Kr26	80% max., Kr18–27	"
1969	Kr587	"	80%, Kr15–20	80% max., Kr15–20	"
1971	Kr731	"	80% max., Kr67	90% max., Kr40–90	"
1973	Kr883	"	as unemployment	90%, Kr106 max.	25–50% for prescriptions
1975	Kr1119	"	"	90%, Kr132 max.	"
1977	Kr1369	"	"	90%, Kr205 max.	"
1979	Kr1804	75%	"	90%, Kr236 max.	"
1981	Kr2098	"	"	90%, Kr274 max.	"
1983	Kr2589	"	"	90%, Kr335 max.	"
1985	Kr2956	"	"	"	"

Source: See table A.7.
a. Amounts in kronen per month for single person; with spouse, plus 50% up to 1975, rising to plus 83% in 1983. Invalidity benefits same as pension.
b. Percentage of earnings for totally disabled through work injury, plus supplements.
c. Amounts in kronen per day. From 1973, same as unemployment benefits.
d. Before 1971, 80% maximum for married person. Amount in kronen per day depending on fund and family situation.

Table A.16
Main features of various benefits for Finland, 1961–1985

Year	Old-age pension[a]	Disability[b]	Sickness[c]	Unemployment[d]	Health care
1961	M29	90% +	–	max. 66⅔% or M10	comprehensive, patient pays 25% laboratory costs, 50% prescriptions
1964	M34	"	M4–22	"	"
1967	M59	"	M5–28	"	comprehensive, patient pays 40% doctor, 25% laboratory costs, 50% prescriptions
1969	M69	"	–	max. 66⅔% or M19	"
1971	M74	"	55% + M8–38	75%, M30	"
1973	M82	"	"	"	"
1975	M112	"	55% + M10–38	75%, M38	"
1977	M153	"	55% + M15–38	75%, M51	"
1979	M175	"	55% + M20–38	75%, M54	"
1981	M215	"	"	75%, M64	"
1983	M268	145% max.	80% + M30 min.	75%, M87	"
1985	M307	"	80% + M37 min.	75%, M70	"

Source: See table A.7.
a. Amounts in markkaa per month for single person; twice that amount with spouse. Invalidity benefits same as pension; extra amounts for dependents.
b. 1981 and before, 60% for total disability due to work injury plus 30% for first dependent, plus 20% for each further dependent. From 1983, 85% generally, plus 60% for total disability.
c. Amounts in markkaa per day plus 15% for first dependent, plus 10% for each further dependent.
d. Percentage of earnings or maximum amount in markkaa per day until 1973. From 1975, M70 per day basic benefit, with supplements.

Table A.17
Main features of various benefits for Norway, 1961–1985

Year	Old-age pension[a]	Disability[b]	Sickness	Unemployment[c]	Health care
1961	Kr2676	60%	as unemployment	Kr3–15	Comprehensive, refund for doctor 66–75%
1964	Kr3780	"	"	Kr3–19	"
1967	Kr5400 + $2\frac{1}{4}$%	"	"	"	"
1969	Kr6400 + $2\frac{1}{4}$%	"	"	Kr6–34	"
1971	Kr7200 + $2\frac{1}{4}$%	100%	"	Kr4 + 36%	"
1973	Kr8500 + $2\frac{1}{4}$%	"	"	"	"
1975	Kr10,400 + $2\frac{1}{4}$%	"	"	Kr15 + 36%	"
1977	Kr13,100 + 45% "difference"	"	100%, Kr440 max.	"	60–100% refund for doctor
1979	Kr15,200 + 45% "difference"	"	"	"	67–100% refund for doctor
1981	Kr17,400 + 45% "difference"	"	100%, Kr521 max.	73%, Kr324 max.	"
1983	Kr21,800 + 45% "difference"	"	100%, Kr618 max.	73%, Kr442 max.	51–100% refund for doctor
1985	Kr24,200 + 45% "difference"	"	100%	73%, Kr310 max.	Kr48 charge for consultations

Source: See table A.7.

a. Flat amount: kroner per year for single person; with spouse, plus 50%. Graduated amount: 1967–1975, percentage of covered earnings × years of coverage, 45% max.; 1977, 45% "difference" between covered earnings and a base amount. Invalidity benefits same as pension.

b. Percentage of earnings for totally disabled through work injury.

c. Amounts in kroner per day for single person; additional amounts for dependents.

Table A.18
Main features of various benefits for Sweden, 1961–1985

Year	Old-age pension[a]	Disability[b]	Sickness[c]	Unemployment[d]	Health care
1961	Kr233 + 60% "difference"	92%	Kr3 + Kr1–13	Kr6–20	Comprehensive, patient pays 20% doctor, 50% prescriptions, partial dental costs
1964	Kr353 + 60% "difference"	"	Kr5 + Kr1–23	"	"
1967	Kr420 + 60% "difference"	"	Kr6 + Kr1–46	Kr12–40	"
1969	Kr450 + 60% "difference"	"	"	Kr18–50	"
1971	Kr480 + 60% "difference"	"	"	"	"
1973	Kr548 + 60% "difference"	"	"	Kr18–60	"
1975	Kr712 + 60% "difference"	"	90%, Kr166 max.	Kr40–130	50% dental costs
1977	Kr847 + 60% "difference"	"	90%, Kr198 max.	Kr50–160	"
1979	Kr1037 + 60% "difference"	100%	90%, Kr242 max.	Kr70–180	"
1981	Kr1274 + 60% "difference"	"	90%, Kr298 max.	Kr80–195	"
1983	Kr1567 + 60% "difference"	"	90%, Kr359 max.	Kr80–280	60% dental costs
1985	Kr1744 + 60% "difference"	"	90%, Kr403 max.	Kr80–300	"

Source: See table A.7.

a. Flat rate element: amounts in kronor per month (with spouse, plus 63%). Earnings-related element is 60% "difference" between the base amount (a little higher than the flat rate element) and annual average earnings. Invalidity benefits same as pension.

b. Percentage of earnings for totally disabled through work injury. Amounts in kronor per year.

c. 1973 and before, amounts in kronor per day. 1975 and after, amounts in kronor per year.

d. Amounts in kronor per day varying with fund and income class.

Table A.19
Main features of various benefits for Austria, 1961–1985

Year	Old-age pension[a]	Disability[b]	Sickness[c]	Unemployment[d]	Health care
1961	30%+	$66\frac{2}{3}$%	50–60%	30–60%	comprehensive, patient pays 20% dentistry; some prescription charges
1964	"	"	"	"	"
1967	"	"	"	"	"
1969	"	"	"	"	"
1971	"	"	"	"	"
1973	"	"	"	"	"
1975	30% + 79.5% max.	"	"	50–100%	"
1977	"	"	"	"	"
1979	"	"	"	"	"
1981	"	"	"	"	"
1983	"	"	"	"	"
1985	1.9%, 79.5% max.	"	"	"	"

Source: See table A.7.

a. Percentage of average earnings of last 5 years, with supplements for years of coverage; 14 payments per year. From 1975, 1.9% average earnings of last 7 years. Invalidity benefits same as pension.

b. For totally disabled through work injury, $66\frac{2}{3}$% of earnings plus supplement of 20% of benefit.

c. 100% of earnings for 4–12 weeks; thereafter 50% with supplements for dependents.

d. Percentage of earnings varying inversely with income, minimum S957 per month, maximum S6192.

Table A.20
Main features of various benefits for Switzerland, 1961−1985

Year	Old-age pension[a]	Disability[b]	Sickness[c]	Unemployment[d]	Health care
1961	Fr29 + (Fr75−154)	70%	Fr1	60−65% + (85% max.)	Comprehensive, patient pays about 10%
1964	Fr83 + (Fr83−277)	"	Fr2	"	"
1967	Fr83 + (Fr138−294)	"	"	"	"
1969	Fr125 + $1\frac{1}{4}\%$ (Fr200−400)	"	"	"	"
1971	Fr125 + $1\frac{1}{4}\%$ (Fr220−440)	"	"	"	"
1973	Fr320 + $1\frac{2}{3}\%$ (Fr400−800)	"	"	"	"
1975	Fr400 + $1\frac{2}{3}\%$ (Fr500−1000)	"	"	65−70% + (85% max.)	"
1977	Fr420 + $1\frac{2}{3}\%$ (Fr525−1050)	"	"	"	"
1979	"	"	"	"	"
1981	Fr440 + $1\frac{2}{3}\%$ (Fr550−1100)	"	"	"	"
1983	Fr496 + 11% (Fr620−1240)	"	"	"	"
1985	Fr552 + 11% (Fr690−1380)	80%	"	75−80%	"

Source: See table A.7.
a. Amounts in francs per month for single person; plus 50% with spouse. Percentage minimum pension plus percentage annual average revalued earnings. Minimum and maximum amounts in parentheses. Invalidity benefits same as pension.
b. Percentage of earnings for totally disabled through work injury.
c. Amounts in francs per day.
d. Lower percentage for single person; higher amounts with dependents.

Table A.21
Main features of various benefits for Ireland, 1961–1985

Year	Old-age pension[a]	Invalidity[b]	Disability[b]	Sickness[b]	Unemployment[b]	Health care
1961	£2	as unemployment	75%	as unemployment	£1.625	comprehensive, some charges
1964	£2.05	"	"	"	£2.125	"
1967	£3	"	£5.75	"	£2.625	"
1969	£4.125	"	£6.25	"	£3.75	"
1971	£6.125	"	£6.25	"	£4.25	"
1973	£6.1	"	£8.1	"	£5.55	"
1975	£8.5	"	£10.8 + 40%	"	£7.75 + 40%	"
1977	£13.9	"	£10.8 + 20–40%	"	£12.45 + 40%	"
1979	£18.6	"	£225 + 20–40%	"	£16.05 + 40%	"
1981	£24.5	£22.05 + 20–40%	£28.2 + 20–40%	"	£20.34 + 20–40%	"
1983	£45.1	£39.75	£47.9 + 20–40%	£31.63 + 20–40%	£34.8 + 20–40%	"
1985	£51.4	£45.3	£54.4 + 20–40%	£39.5 + 20–40%	£39.5 + 20–40%	"

Source: See table A.7.
a. Amounts in pounds per week for single person; for married person, 64% higher.
b. From 1977 onward graduated element was 20–40% times income in the range of £14 to £140 per week (1981); for 1975, 40% difference between flat amount benefit and actual earnings.

Table A.22
Main features of various benefits for Spain, 1961–1985

Year	Old-age pension[a]	Invalidity[b]	Disability	Sickness[c]	Unemployment[d]	Health care
1961	Pta400	as pension	75–100%	50%	75%	comprehensive but hospitalization limited
1964	Pta1000 min.	"	"	"	"	"
1967	"	"	"	75%	"	"
1969	25% + 1%	55%	55%	"	"	patient shares prescription costs
1971	"	"	"	"	"	"
1973	"	"	100% max.	100% max.	"	"
1975	"	"	"	"	"	"
1977	50% + 2%	"	"	"	"	"
1979	"	"	"	"	"	"
1981	"	"	"	60–75%	60–80%, max. 220% min. wage	comprehensive, patient pays 40% for medicine
1983	"	"	"	"	"	"
1985	"	"	"	"	"	"

Source: See table A.7.

a. 50% of earnings in pesetas per month of highest 2 of last 7 years, plus 2% × years of contribution from 11 to 35 years, maximum 100%.

b. For total invalidity, 100% earnings up to contribution ceiling.

c. 60% of earnings up to 21 days; 75% thereafter.

d. Percentage of earnings for 6 months, declining to 70% for second 6 months, 60% for third 6 months.

Table A.23
Main features of various benefits for Greece, 1961–1985

Year	Old-age pension[a]	Disability	Sickness	Unemployment	Health care
1961	80% min. wage + graduated element	as pension	50%	40–50%	comprehensive patient pays up to 25%
1964	28–98% of earnings	"	"	"	"
1967	"	"	"	"	"
1969	"	"	"	"	"
1971	"	"	"	"	"
1973	"	"	"	"	"
1975	$32–70\% + 1–2\frac{1}{3}\%$	"	"	"	"
1977	$30–70\% + 2\frac{1}{2}\%$	"	"	"	"
1979	"	"	"	"	"
1981	$30–70\% + 1–2\frac{1}{2}\%$	"	"	"	"
1983	"	"	"	"	"
1985	"	"	"	"	"

Source: See table A.7.
a. Percentage varies inversely with income, supplementary $1–2\frac{1}{2}\%$ for each 300 days beyond 3000 days. Invalidity benefits same as pension.

Table A.24
Main features of various benefits for Portugal, 1961–1985

Year	Old-age pension[a]	Disability[b]	Sickness	Unemployment[c]	Health care
1961	20% + 2%	66⅔%	60%	$40–100	comprehensive, patients share 50% in costs after 1 free year
1964	"	"	"	"	"
1967	"	"	"	"	"
1969	"	"	"	"	"
1971	"	"	"	"	"
1973	"	"	"	"	"
1975	2%	"	"	"	"
1977	"	"	"	50% min. wage	"
1979	"	"	"	60% min. wage	"
1981	"	66⅔ min.	" wage or 50%	"	"
1983	"	"	"	70% min. wage	"
1985	2.2%	"	"	"	"

Source: See table A.7.
a. From 1975, 2% × years of coverage × highest 5 of last 10 years revalued earnings; minimum 30%, maximum 70%. Invalidity benefits same as pension.
b. For totally disabled through work injury.
c. Highest percentage for married person, duration 6 months plus possible 6 months extension.

Table A.25
Evolution of public expenditure on social programs as percentage of GDP[a]

Year and benefit	Belgium	Denmark	Germany	France	Ireland	Italy	Luxem-bourg	The Nether-lands	United Kingdom	European Community[b]
1970										
Health care, sickness	3.8	5.6	5.7	4.9	4.1	—	2.7	5.7	3.9	5.0
Invalidity and work accidents	2.2	2.7	2.6	1.8	1.3	—	2.9	3.1	1.2	2.1
Pensions	7.1	6.9	9.4	7.5	4.6	—	7.8	7.7	6.7	7.9
Maternity and family	3.5	2.7	2.1	3.1	2.3	—	1.8	2.6	1.5	2.3
Unemployment	0.6	0.4	0.1	0.3	0.4	—	0.0	0.6	0.3	0.3
Other	0.0	0.1	0.3	0.0	0.1	—	0.0	0.8	0.1	0.2
Total	17.4	19.0	20.7	18.2	13.3	—	15.4	19.0	13.8	18.0
1983										
Health care, sickness	6.5	7.1	7.5	6.8	8.4	5.7	11.1	8.4	4.7	6.7
Invalidity and work accidents	3.3	2.6	3.1	2.3	—	5.4	—	6.4	2.2	2.9
Pensions	11.5	10.4	12.1	11.2	7.4	11.5	12.0	10.3	9.8	11.1
Maternity and family	3.0	3.1	2.0	3.1	—	2.0	1.2	2.7	2.8	2.6
Unemployment	4.2	4.1	2.0	2.7	—	0.8	0.0	4.2	2.3	2.5
Other	0.5	1.1	0.6	0.2	3.1	0.0	0.8	0.0	0.3	0.4
Total	29.5	30.1	27.8	27.4	23.2	25.5	25.5	32.7	23.1	27.0

Table A.25 (continued)

Year and benefit	Belgium	Denmark	Germany	France	Ireland	Italy	Luxem-bourg	The Nether-lands	United Kingdom	European Community[b]
Increase, 1970 to 1983										
Health care, sickness	2.7	1.5	1.8	1.9	4.3	—	8.4	2.7	0.8	1.7
Invalidity and work accidents	1.1	−0.1	0.5	0.5	—	—	—	3.3	1.0	0.8
Pensions	4.4	3.5	2.7	3.7	2.8	—	4.2	2.6	3.1	3.1
Maternity and family	−0.5	0.4	−0.1	0.0	—	—	−0.6	0.1	1.3	0.2
Unemployment	3.6	3.7	1.9	2.4	3.0	—	0.0	3.6	2.0	2.3
Other	0.5	1.0	0.3	0.2	—	—	0.8	−0.8	0.2	0.2
Total	12.1	11.1	7.1	9.2	9.9	—	10.1	13.7	9.3	9.0

Source: EUROSTAT, "European System of Social Protection Statistics," Data File.

a. For Italy, total public expenditure increased from 34.2% of GDP to 57.1% in 1973, a 22.9% point increase; this compares with a 13.4% increase for the European Community as a whole. Although statistics on social programs in Italy in 1970 are lacking, it is likely that the increase in such expenditures from 1970 to 1983 was greater in Italy, as a share of GDP, than in any other European Community country.

b. European Community excluding Italy.

Appendix B

Econometric Model Simulation of a Medium-Term Scenario for a Reduction of Unemployment in the European Community

André Dramais

The macroeconomics of the strategy outlined in chapter 4 has been tested with the aid of some simulations performed on an econometric model of the European Community.

The model in question (COMPACT) has been described in detail elsewhere (Dramais 1986). A summary of the main features of this model is given in section B.1. Then a presentation of the behavioral properties of the model, notably where they feature importantly in the simulation of the medium-term scenario for reducing unemployment, is given in section B.2. This is done through showing separately the results of several components of the strategy (for example, changes in social security taxes, public investment, wage increases, monetary expansion, and exchange rate depreciation). Finally, the simulation itself is described precisely, in terms of both the measures introduced and the results. Although these results are given in some detail in table B.7, it should be stressed that an econometric model of the type used cannot, as is explained in what follows, fully represent all aspects of the scenario.

B.1 Main Features of the COMPACT Model of the Economy of the European Community

The COMPACT world model is based on a decomposition of the world economy into three behavioral models for the European

Community as a whole, the United States, and Japan. The system is completed by a rest-of-world module, which is mostly determined as a residual item in order to ensure accounting consistency at the world level for international trade and capital flows.

The European Community module is somewhat stylized. It includes, however, all the basic elements of a macroeconomic model: a final demand block, a production and factor demand block, a wage and price block, a public sector block, a monetary block, and a linkage and balance-of-payments block.

Leaving aside the trade linkage part, the European Community model includes fifty endogenous variables determined by twenty-eight behavioral equations and twenty-two identities. The estimation is done on yearly data. The United States and Japan modules were derived from existing material, that is, from the world model built by the Economic Planning Agency (EPA) of the Japanese government. After analytical reduction these two models were compacted from about seventy behavioral relations to eighteen equations, the coefficients of which are combinations of the initial published parameters.

The rest-of-world module includes only international trade and capital variables and an estimate of its GDP. In this module current and capital account balances are determined so as to implement world consistency, that is, to constrain current and capital world balances to sum to 0.

The main features of the European Community module are:

1. the attention paid to both stock and flow equilibrium in the flow of funds matrix between economic agents, viz. households, enterprises, public authorities, and the foreign sector;

2. the inclusion of wealth effects in consumers' demand;

3. the disaggregation of total unemployment among classical, Keynesian, and frictional shares using a labor market disequilibrium approach;

4. the integration of the balance-of-payments item with the

determination of the public sector borrowing requirement and money supply;

5. the integration of the distinction between Keynesian and classical unemployment into the wage determination process and, via wages, into the inflation process.

The structure of the various blocks may be described as follows.

Aggregate Supply and Demand Conditions

The aggregate European Community model uses a production frontier of the CES (constant elasticity of substitution) type for the derivation of labor demand relations. The production frontier itself is used to derive target levels for potential employment and output, subject to a given capital stock. The targets are the potential level of aggregate supply compatible with full employment of the capital stock and potential labor demand in the sense of Sneessens (1983), that is, the maximum quantity of labor that firms are ready to hire, dependent on both capital stock and real factor costs.

Aggregate demand (excluding inventories) is determined in the usual way as the sum of private and public consumption, fixed investment, and net exports. Private consumption includes both income and wealth effects, which gives a direct feedback from the monetary sector to the real sector. The determination of fixed investment also takes into account monetary variables (that is, the long-term real interest rate) in the definition of capital user costs. This is compared to the marginal product of capital, which is equal in long-run equilibrium to its real rate of return, hence establishing a linkage with profitability conditions. Net exports are determined in the linkage part.

With a given level of aggregate demand, inventories and prices fluctuate in order to ensure ex post short-run equilibrium between aggregate supply and demand on the goods market.

On the labor market side the approach follows Sneessens (1986) and Sneessens and Drèze (1986), that is, effective observed labor demand (L) is defined as the minimum of (1) potential demand (LP), that is, the maximum amount firms are ready to hire, given the existing capital stock and factor costs; (2) "Keynesian" demand (LK), defined as a log-linear function of final demand and the relative cost of labor, together with terms of trade effects; and (3) labor supply (LS), defined as a log-linear function of active population. These elements are combined with an adaptive adjustment lag in order to take into account labor market rigidities; in log-linear form:

$$\log L = a \min(\log LP, \log LK, \log LS) + (1 - a)\log L_{-1} + u,$$

$$PA_t = pa_t \cdot PWA_t,$$

where PA is the active population (employment and unemployment), PWA is the population in the working-age group, and pa_t is the average participation rate.

In the simulation reported here the labor participation rate is treated exogenously. The constant in the relation between LS and PA takes into account frictional unemployment. The feedback to the rest of the model goes through the wage equation.

According to the production block formulation, long-run consistency implies that equilibrium real wage costs should be determined by equilibrium real labor productivity and the elasticity of substitution:

$$\log W_r^* = \text{constant} + 1/s \log plr^*,$$

where s is the CES elasticity of substitution.

For empirical applications there should be adjustment lags, as in the labor demand formulation. The length of the adjustment lag is influenced by the degree of pressure on the labor market measured by the share of Keynesian unemployment in total unemployment. In other words, when unemployment is inherently of a classical nature (with therefore a low share of Keynesian unemployment), the relation between real wage cost per person employed and real productivity per person employed still works as if the unemployment rate were low.

Prices and Incomes

The approach for price inflation is based on the microeconomic approach to average cost pricing. The domestic deflator is linked to expected average cost, as given by the production block through an adjustment lag. It also uses "surprises" in the form of increases in the rate of variation of the import price and the money stock (giving therefore a second-order equation) and also of variations in the pressure of demand indicator defined as the ratio of potential capital output, as computed in the production block, to total demand minus imports.

The consumption and investment prices are linked to the domestic deflator, with a terms of trade effect. Disposable income is reconciled with the financial constraints and is defined as the sum of the wage bill, interest, and dividend income on domestic private and public bonds and on foreign bonds.

Government Sector

Most relations in the government sector block are identities, using average tax rates, etc. as policy variables on the income side. On the expenditure side the main variables are fixed exogenously, either in real or nominal terms, according to the kind of policy scenario introduced in the model.

Similarly, the interest on public debt is accounted for by an identity using an average rate of return concept. This average rate of return (total of interest paid divided by the stock of debt at the beginning of the period) is then linked to short- and long-term interest rates through a Koyck lag.

Monetary and Financial Relations

As mentioned before, behavioral relations are needed for all asset demands not given by identities. Money demand (M_2/M_3)
is determined as a function of nominal income (the transaction
motive), short-term interest rates (as proxy for the yield of
interest-bearing elements in M_2/M_3), and long-term interest
rates (as proxy for alternative asset yields). The stock of foreign
reserves is either exogenous or endogenous, according to the
exchange rate determination model.

The exchange rate (measured as the ECU/$ rate) comes
from the balance-of-payments identity, according to the "Flex"
approach proposed by Amano et al. (1983). In simulation
exercises the exchange rate is either fixed exogenously, with
international reserves fluctuating in order to maintain the
balance-of-payments identity, or left free to fluctuate in order to
make the current and capital balance changes equal and of
opposite sign (with no changes in international reserves). In the
simulations set out later, some exogenous setting of the exchange rate has been made (notably for tables B.4 and B.7).

Net assets of the private sector are determined through the
private sector balance sheet. There remains therefore the net
foreign assets position. The equation used is a standard stock
allocation relationship from a modified portfolio adjustment
function. The ratio of the net capital inflow (or outflow, according to sign) to the net foreign assets stock at the beginning of
the period is a function of (1) the rate of change in net foreign
assets; (2) the level of and change in the difference between
domestic and foreign yields, as measured by domestic and
foreign interest rates, given the exchange rate (for simplicity
the forward premium is implicitly constant); (3) an expectation
factor on the exchange rate measured as the discrepancy between the rate of change in the exchange rate and the difference
between domestic and foreign inflation rates, as an attempt to

measure the influence of expectations about future PPP-driven exchange rate movements; and (4) the current balance, as a share of net foreign assets (matching credit creation to finance trade, plus active search of capital inflows or outflows to offset current account deficits or surpluses).

So far as the government position is concerned, when a distinction between domestic and foreign debt is included, an equation is needed for distribution between the two. The ratio of domestic debt to total debt is a function of the existing debt to GDP ratio, the expected growth in the money stock, and variations in real long-term interest rates, domestic and foreign. Finally, the variation in the share of new domestic debt in new total public debt feeds back into the term structure equation for the long-term rate, together with the US rate for the non-US zones.

B.2   Basic Multiplier Tables

Tables B.1 to B.6 contain an indication of the individual impact of the policy measures incorporated into the composite scenario. Each measure (or "shock") is thus applied in isolation, all other policy instruments being held constant. Given nonlinearities in the behavior of the model, the composite scenario is not strictly equal to the sum of its components. The tables make it easier, however, to see where the main impacts are coming from.

For comparability all measures are given in a standardized form with shocks introduced as a percent of baseline GDP in the first year and sustained at that level over five years in order to show the development of dynamic effects. All budgetary measures are made with a nonaccommodating (fixed money supply) monetary policy and floating exchange rates. A full description of the shocks can be found in Dramais (1986), but the main results can be described as follows.

Table B.1
Autonomous increase in public investment, by 1% of baseline GDP, sustained over five years, for the European Community (ten countries)[a]

Component	Year 1	Year 2	Year 3	Year 4	Year 5
Real GDP	1.1	1.3	0.9	0.6	0.5
Nominal GDP	1.3	1.6	1.8	1.9	2.2
Real private consumption	0.2	0.4	0.3	0.2	0.2
Real private investment	0.9	1.4	1.1	0.5	−0.4
Real exports	−0.2	−0.4	−0.6	−0.7	−0.9
Real imports	1.3	1.6	1.4	1.0	0.9
GDP deflator	0.2	0.3	0.9	1.3	1.7
Consumption deflator	0.2	0.4	1.0	1.4	1.8
Export deflator (in ECU)	0.1	0.3	0.8	1.0	1.4
Import deflator (in ECU)	0.0	0.1	0.2	0.3	0.3
Real labor productivity	0.8	0.9	0.6	0.5	0.4
Real wage-cost rate	0.1	0.4	0.9	1.0	1.3
Total employment	0.3	0.4	0.3	0.1	0.0
Unemployment rate[b]	−0.3	−0.4	−0.3	−0.1	0.0
Budget deficit (% GDP)[b]	−0.9	−0.7	−0.6	−0.6	−0.7
Current balance (% GDP)[b]	−0.3	−0.6	−0.5	−0.4	−0.4
Long-term interest rate[c]	0.4	0.7	1.2	1.7	2.2
Exchange rate (ECU/$)	0.1	0.3	0.4	0.4	0.5
Wage share in GDP[b]	−0.6	−0.5	0.3	0.5	0.9
Real gross operating surplus	3.5	2.9	0.1	−1.0	−2.3

a. The figures show the relative discrepancy with respect to baseline levels, in percent except when noted.
b. Differences in percentage points with respect to baseline level.
c. Cumulated changes in interest rate levels, in percentage points.

Public Investment Shock

The public investment shock (table B.1), with an increase in such expenditures, has positive effects on economic output in the short term. In the medium term (from year 3 on) the model generates a strong crowding-out of private expenditures and most notably private investment, given the inflationary pressures and increases in nominal and real interest rates and the deterioration of net exports. After five years these negative feedbacks completely cancel the initial gain in employment, and the unemployment rate is back to its baseline level.

Social Security Contribution

The cut in the social security contribution (table B.2) exhibits some "virtuous circle" characteristics: (1) It causes an increase in Keynesian labor demand through real income and wealth effects, compatible with the increase in potential labor demand. Indeed, it is in the logic of the disequilibrium approach of the labor market that both actual and potential labor demand should increase if a significant acceleration of labor demand is to be obtained. (2) With a lag the social security contribution also increases the expected supply of output in the economy. This in turn ensures the acceleration of investment needed to sustain potential labor demand in the long run, once the changes in factor prices are absorbed. The resulting expansion of productive capacity will also help to contain demand-pull inflationary pressures.

A complex process of supply-demand interactions is thus put into motion, leading to a new equilibrium position with higher GDP, higher employment and capital stock, and a higher share of profits and a lower share of wages in value added, lower prices, and lower interest rate levels. This simulation indicates low productivity gains (if any), which helps to limit claims for real wage increases despite the reduction in unemployment.

Table B.2
Autonomous decrease in employers' social security contributions by 1% of baseline GDP, sustained over five years, for the European Community (ten countries)[a]

Component	Year 1	Year 2	Year 3	Year 4	Year 5
Real GDP	0.3	0.5	0.9	1.3	1.5
Nominal GDP	− 0.4	− 0.7	− 0.4	0.0	0.1
Real private consumption	0.2	0.4	0.8	1.0	1.1
Real private investment	0.3	0.8	2.2	3.1	4.2
Real exports	0.3	0.7	0.9	1.1	1.2
Real imports	0.0	0.2	0.7	1.1	1.3
GDP deflator	− 0.7	− 1.2	− 1.3	− 1.3	− 1.4
Consumption deflator	− 0.5	− 1.0	− 1.2	− 1.2	− 1.3
Export deflator (in ECU)	− 0.5	− 0.9	− 1.0	− 1.1	− 1.2
Import deflator (in ECU)	0.0	+ 0.1	+ 0.2	+ 0.4	+ 0.5
Real labor productivity	0.2	− 0.1	− 0.1	− 0.1	− 0.2
Real wage-cost rate	− 1.1	− 0.6	− 0.5	− 0.7	− 0.7
Total employment	0.1	0.6	1.0	1.4	1.7
Unemployment rate[b]	− 0.1	− 0.5	− 0.9	− 1.3	− 1.5
Budget deficit (% GDP)[b]	− 0.9	− 0.7	− 0.5	− 0.3	− 0.1
Current balance (% GDP)[b]	− 0.1	− 0.2	− 0.3	− 0.2	− 0.2
Long-term interest rate[c]	− 0.2	− 0.7	− 0.9	− 1.0	− 1.1
Exchange rate (ECU/$)	+ 0.1	+ 0.2	+ 0.2	+ 0.3	+ 0.4
Wage share in GDP[b]	− 1.0	− 0.4	− 0.4	− 0.6	− 0.5
Real gross operating surplus	4.3	2.1	2.5	3.7	3.5

a. The figures show the relative discrepancy with respect to baseline levels, in percent except when noted.
b. Differences in percentage points with respect to baseline level.
c. Cumulated changes in interest rate levels, in percentage points.

The major constraint comes from the balance of payments, which deteriorates because of negative terms of trade effects and because the strong induced demand causes imports to grow faster than exports once price differentials are stabilized.

For public finances the expansion of the economy and the fall in unemployment and interest rates leads to a full offset by the end of the five-year period of the initial ex ante cut in public receipts.

Monetary Expansion

The monetary expansion (table B.3) has a weak impact on real GDP but a strong nominal influence. When the five-year period (shown in the table) is extended by one or two more years, nominal GDP reaches a level that is 1% above baseline, as with the exogenously set money supply level, but real GDP goes back to its baseline level.

Devaluation

The devaluation simulation (table B.4) shows a rise in domestic prices following the increases in import costs and a rise in real net exports. Domestic demand, however, is negatively influenced initially by real income and wealth effects. Domestic absorption therefore reduces the positive contribution of net exports to GDP growth. The current balance is influenced by adverse J-curve effects during the first year but improves afterward.

Wage Moderation

The wage moderation exercises (tables B.5 and B.6) are strongly influenced by the structure of the model and the explicit distinction between "Keynesian" and "classical" labor demand. A comparison of table B.5 with table B.2 shows, for instance,

Table B.3
Money supply expansion, with money supply growth kept autonomously one percentage point above the baseline nominal GDP growth for the European Community (ten countries)[a]

Component	Year 1	Year 2	Year 3	Year 4	Year 5
Real GDP	0.2	0.3	0.4	0.4	0.2
Nominal GDP	0.3	0.7	1.0	1.2	1.1
Real private consumption	0.2	0.3	0.5	0.5	0.3
Real private investment	0.0	0.1	0.3	0.4	0.2
Real exports	−0.0	−0.1	−0.2	−0.4	−0.6
Real imports	0.3	0.4	0.6	0.7	0.5
GDP deflator	0.2	0.4	0.6	0.8	0.9
Consumption deflator	0.3	0.5	0.8	1.0	1.0
Export deflator (in ECU)	0.2	0.2	0.3	0.2	0.2
Import deflator (in ECU)	0.2	0.4	0.8	1.2	1.5
Real labor productivity	0.1	0.2	0.2	0.2	0.1
Real wage-cost rate	0.0	0.1	0.2	0.2	0.3
Total employment	0.1	0.1	0.2	0.2	0.1
Unemployment rate[b]	−0.1	−0.1	−0.2	−0.2	−0.1
Budget deficit (% GDP)[b]	0.1	0.2	0.3	0.4	0.4
Current balance (% GDP)[b]	−0.1	−0.1	−0.2	−0.2	−0.3
Long-term interest rate[c]	−0.2	−0.3	−0.4	−0.5	−0.4
Exchange rate (ECU/$)	0.4	0.6	1.0	1.5	1.8
Wage share in GDP[b]	−0.1	−0.1	0.0	0.0	0.2
Real gross operating surplus	0.4	0.4	0.0	0.0	−0.8

a. The figures show the relative discrepancy with respect to baseline levels, in percent except when noted.
b. Differences in percentage points with respect to baseline level.
c. Cumulated changes in interest rate levels, in percentage points.

Table B.4
Autonomous devaluation of the ECU by 10% with respect to baseline, sustained over five years, for the European Community (ten countries)[a]

Component	Year 1	Year 2	Year 3	Year 4	Year 5
Real GDP	+ 0.1	+ 0.3	+ 0.5	+ 0.4	+ 0.3
Nominal GDP	+ 0.9	+ 1.5	+ 2.1	+ 2.2	+ 2.2
Real private consumption	− 0.5	− 0.6	− 0.4	− 0.2	0.0
Real private investment	+ 0.1	+ 0.2	+ 0.5	+ 0.4	+ 0.4
Real exports	+ 1.5	+ 1.7	+ 1.6	+ 1.5	+ 1.3
Real imports	− 1.4	− 2.6	− 2.3	− 2.1	− 1.9
GDP deflator	+ 0.8	+ 1.2	+ 1.6	+ 1.8	+ 1.8
Consumption deflator	+ 1.2	+ 2.0	+ 2.2	+ 2.3	+ 2.3
Export deflator (in ECU)	+ 2.3	+ 4.1	+ 5.2	+ 5.3	+ 5.3
Import deflator (in ECU)	+ 5.1	+ 6.2	+ 6.9	+ 7.1	+ 7.0
Real labor productivity	0.0	− 0.1	+ 0.2	0.0	+ 0.1
Real wage-cost rate	− 0.1	0.0	+ 0.1	+ 0.1	+ 0.2
Total employment	+ 0.1	+ 0.2	+ 0.3	+ 0.4	+ 0.3
Unemployment rate[b]	− 0.1	− 0.2	− 0.3	− 0.4	− 0.3
Budget deficit (% GDP)[b]	− 0.1	− 0.1	0.0	+ 0.0	+ 0.1
Current balance (% GDP)[b]	0.0	+ 0.3	+ 0.4	+ 0.4	+ 0.3
Long-term interest rate[c]	+ 0.5	+ 1.0	+ 1.6	+ 2.0	+ 2.2
Exchange rate (ECU/$)	10.0	10.0	10.0	10.0	10.0
Wage share in GDP[b]	− 0.1	0.0	0.0	+ 0.1	+ 0.1
Real gross operating surplus	+ 0.5	+ 0.3	+ 0.5	0.0	− 0.1

a. The figures show the relative discrepancy with respect to baseline levels, in percent except when noted.
b. Differences in percentage points with respect to baseline level.
c. Cumulated changes in interest rate levels, in percentage points.

Table B.5
Nominal wages per employee kept 4% below baseline, over five years, without demand support, for European Community (ten countries)[a]

Component	Year 1	Year 2	Year 3	Year 4	Year 5
Real GDP	−0.8	−0.2	0.1	0.4	0.6
Nominal GDP	−2.2	−2.7	−2.6	−2.3	−2.2
Real private consumption	−1.0	−1.0	−0.8	−0.4	−0.1
Real private investment	−0.4	−0.2	1.8	2.6	3.6
Real exports	0.4	0.9	1.2	1.4	1.5
Real imports	−0.5	−1.2	−0.7	−0.2	0.2
GDP deflator	−1.4	−2.5	−2.6	−2.7	−2.8
Consumption deflator	−1.3	−2.3	−2.5	−2.6	−2.6
Export deflator (in ECU)	−1.0	−1.8	−2.0	−2.2	−2.2
Import deflator (in ECU)	−0.1	−0.2	−0.2	−0.3	−0.3
Real labor productivity	−0.6	−0.1	−0.3	−0.6	−0.7
Real wage-cost rate	−2.6	−1.5	−1.4	−1.3	−1.2
Total employment	−0.2	−0.2	0.4	1.0	1.3
Unemployment rate[b]	0.2	0.2	−0.3	−0.9	−1.1
Budget deficit (% GDP)[b]	−0.2	−0.2	0.0	0.2	0.3
Current balance (% GDP)[b]	0.2	0.2	0.2	0.2	0.2
Long-term interest rate[c]	−0.5	−1.0	−1.5	−2.2	−2.4
Exchange rate (ECU/$)	−0.3	−0.4	−0.4	−0.5	−0.5
Wage share in GDP[b]	−1.5	−1.1	−0.8	−0.6	−0.5
Real gross operating surplus	5.3	4.2	3.3	2.6	2.5

a. The figures show the relative discrepancy with respect to baseline levels, in percent except when noted.
b. Differences in percentage points with respect to baseline level.
c. Cumulated changes in interest rate levels, in percentage points.

Table B.6
Nominal wages per employee kept 4% below baseline, over five years, with public expenditure increases sufficient to keep nominal GDP at baseline level for the European Community (ten countries)[a]

Component	1986	1987	1988	1989	1990
Real GDP	1.0	1.6	2.3	2.6	2.7
Nominal GDP	0.0	0.0	0.0	0.0	0.0
Real private consumption	−0.6	−0.2	0.5	1.3	1.7
Real private investment	0.6	2.1	2.8	3.4	4.7
Real exports	0.5	1.6	1.9	2.0	2.0
Real imports	0.6	1.8	2.3	2.5	2.6
GDP deflator	−1.0	−1.6	−2.3	−2.6	−2.7
Consumption deflator	−0.9	−1.4	−2.2	−2.4	−2.6
Export deflator (in ECU)	−0.7	−1.1	−1.8	−2.0	−2.2
Import deflator (in ECU)	0.1	0.2	0.3	0.4	0.5
Real labor productivity	0.8	0.4	−0.1	−0.8	−0.9
Real wage-cost rate	−3.0	−2.4	−1.7	−1.4	−1.3
Total employment	0.2	1.2	2.4	3.4	3.6
Unemployment rate[b]	−0.2	−1.1	−2.2	−3.1	−3.2
Budget deficit (% GDP)[b]	−1.0	−0.5	−0.2	0.2	0.4
Current balance (% GDP)[b]	−0.2	−0.5	−0.5	−0.4	−0.4
Long-term interest rate[c]	−0.3	−0.8	−1.4	−1.8	−2.0
Exchange rate (ECU/$)	0.2	0.2	0.3	0.4	0.6
Wage share in GDP[b]	−2.8	−2.1	−1.2	−0.5	−0.3
Real gross operating surplus	12.2	9.9	8.7	5.1	4.0

a. The figures show the relative discrepancy with respect to baseline levels, in percent except when noted.
b. Differences in percentage points with respect to baseline level.
c. Cumulated changes in interest rate levels, in percentage points.

that a cut in wages is less efficient in reducing unemployment than a cut in social security taxes, even when both lead to the same reduction in wage cost. This is because wage cuts affect private consumption in a way that reduces potential supply expectations and hence investment.

In both wage simulations nominal wages are in the first year brought to a level that is 4% below that contained in the baseline projection, and this margin is held constant over the following four years. The difference between the two simulations (in tables B.5 and B.6) concerns whether an active demand policy accompanies the wage policy. In the first case demand policy is passive, and there is a tendency for demand to be depressed in the early years of the simulation period. In the second case demand policy (budgetary in this case) is calibrated year by year so as to maintain the evolution of total nominal demand (or nominal GDP) on the same path as is in the baseline projection. In this case the problem of temporary demand depression is avoided. The overall result then becomes similar to the simulation of reduced security taxes, with the same "virtuous circle" characteristics, that is, the generation of a self-supporting expansion of demand and supply.

B.3   Definition of the Employment-Creating Growth Strategy

The employment-intensive growth strategy used in chapter 4 is defined with respect to a baseline projection for a seven-year period. This period may be assumed to begin in the late 1980s. The baseline projection roughly portrays an extrapolation of current medium-term trends and policies in the European Community. The baseline projection is based on the behavior of the COMPACT model of the European Community. This projection sees an average rate of growth of about 2.6% for GDP and 0.6% for labor demand. Because of the substantial fall in the growth of the population of working age and to the near-stability of the labor force participation rate, the unemployment rate falls slowly from 10.5% to 8.5%. This development could hardly be judged satisfactory and is in any case vulnerable to any recovery of the participation rate from its present all-time low level. Should, for instance, the participation rate return to 70%, then the unemployment rate would jump to 14% and more by the end of the period, all other things being equal.

As regards the international environment, the most critical assumption is the evolution of oil prices, which stay around $15 per barrel in the initial years of the projection, rising later to $22.

The employment-creating growth strategy is based on a marked reduction in the level of unit wage cost, together with temporary fiscal and monetary stimuli aimed at supporting demand at the beginning of the period, when the expected dynamic supply-side effects are still weak. More specifically: (1) Social security contributions of employers are cut by 1% of baseline GDP per year, cumulatively, during the first four years and by a further 0.5% in the fifth year, making a total ex ante reduction of 4.5% of GDP in five years, that is, a cumulative reduction in nominal wage cost per capita levels of about 8.6% ex ante. (2) In order to reinforce the impact of these social security measures on wage costs, wage earners accept during the first two years a growth of nominal gross wages of 2% per year less than in the baseline projection, that is, 4% cumulatively. The baseline rate of growth of gross nominal wages is about 4.5% in the first two years, that is, 9.3% cumulatively. The 4% reduction therefore maintains an increase in nominal disposable wages, sufficient in fact to keep *real* disposable wages growth slightly positive during the first two years of the scenario. (3) Public investment and money supply are increased temporarily in order to sustain overall demand, offsetting the deflationary impact of the wage moderation (nominal GDP grows 6% in the scenario on average for the whole period, compared to 5.6% in the baseline projection). (4) The exchange

Table B.7
Summary of growth strategy components

Component	Year 1	Year 2	Year 3	Year 4	Year 5	Year 6	Year 7
Social security contributions, employers (% of GDP)	−1.0	−2.0	−3.0	−4.0	−4.5	−4.5	−4.5
Nominal wage moderation (% of wage level)	−2.0	−4.0	−4.0	−4.0	−4.0	−4.0	−4.0
Public investment (% of GDP)	0.6	1.3	1.5	1.4	1.0	0.4	0.0
Money supply expansion (% above nominal GDP growth)	1.3	2.0	1.0	1.0	1.0	1.0	1.0
Exchange rate ECU/$ (+ = devaluation)	5	10	10	10	10	10	10

rate ECU/$ depreciates by 5% in the first two years, in order to limit the deterioration of the trade balance.

Table B.7 summarizes the components of the scenario, giving the precise figures (in cumulative percentage discrepancies with respect to the baseline levels, ex ante).

B.4   Main Results

Table B.8 gives the main results of the baseline (B) and the scenario (S). For the seven-year period as a whole, an annual growth rate of GDP of 4% is achieved in the scenario, compared to 2.6% in the baseline projection. The initial growth impetus is provided principally by private and public investment and, to a lesser extent, exports. The investment boom is due to (1) the substantial increase in profitability coming from the fall in wage costs, (2) the accelerator effect of the demand support through public investment and exports, and (3) the fall in real interest rates resulting from the monetary expansion. Exports react to the improvement of relative labor costs and the devaluation of the ECU. From the third year on, private consumption complements exports and investment because of the strong growth of disposable wage income (disposable wages being no more affected by wage moderation from the third year on).

In the medium to long run the model converges toward a new stable growth path, with GDP, capital stock (that is, *net* investment), and private consumption all growing at 3.5% per annum at the end of the simulation period. Labor demand expands strongly, because of both the cut in wage costs and the expansion of productive capacity (thus increasing "classical" increasing "Keynesian" labor demand). For the seven-year period the annual growth of total employment is 2.1%. The unemployment rate declines to about 5% at the end of the period, despite a substantial increase in the participation rate.

Table B.8

Main macroeconomic results for the baseline projection (B) and the employment-creating scenario (S) for the European Community (ten countries)[a]

Variable	Year 1 B	Year 1 S	Year 2 B	Year 2 S	Year 3 B	Year 3 S	Year 4 B	Year 4 S	Year 5 B	Year 5 S	Year 6 B	Year 6 S	Year 7 B	Year 7 S	Seven-year annual average B	Seven-year annual average S
Real GDP	2.8	3.9	2.6	4.4	2.5	4.3	2.5	4.2	2.5	3.9	2.5	3.5	2.5	3.5	2.6	4.0
Nominal GDP	5.9	6.5	5.6	6.3	5.4	5.9	5.5	6.0	5.5	5.9	5.5	5.6	5.5	5.5	5.6	6.0
GDP deflator	3.1	2.6	3.0	1.9	2.8	1.6	3.0	1.8	3.0	2.0	3.0	2.1	3.0	2.0	3.0	2.0
Labor demand	0.8	1.0	0.7	2.1	0.6	3.0	0.5	2.9	0.5	2.4	0.5	2.0	0.5	1.6	0.6	2.1
Unemployment rate (% of active labor force)	10.5	11.0	10.7	10.5	9.8	9.1	9.5	7.8	9.2	6.8	8.9	5.4	8.5	4.5		
Participation rate (% of population of working age)	65.9	66.5	66.0	67.4	66.1	68.3	66.2	69.2	66.3	70.0	66.4	70.6	66.5	71.0		
Productivity	2.0	2.9	1.9	2.3	2.0	1.3	2.0	1.3	2.0	1.5	2.0	1.5	2.0	1.9	2.0	1.9
Real wage cost (deflated by GDP deflator)	1.4	−1.2	1.6	−0.1	2.0	1.1	2.1	1.6	1.8	1.5	1.9	1.5	2.0	1.7	1.8	0.9
Real disposable wage (deflated by the CPI)	1.9	0.4	1.7	1.1	1.7	2.5	1.8	3.2	1.6	2.4	1.9	1.5	2.0	1.7	1.8	1.8
Real wage cost per unit of output	−0.6	−4.1	−0.3	−2.4	0.0	−0.2	0.1	0.3	−0.2	0.0	−0.1	0.0	0.0	−0.2	−0.2	−1.0
Net lending (+) or borrowing (−) of general government (% of GDP)	−4.0	−5.0	−3.8	−5.6	−3.1	−5.4	−2.7	−4.9	−2.4	−3.8	−2.2	−2.9	−2.0	−2.0		

Current balance (% of GDP)	0.8	0.7	0.7	0.3	0.1	−0.6	−0.1	−1.0	0.0	−1.0	0.1	−0.8	0.2	−0.6	
Long-term interest rate (%)	7.6	7.3	7.5	6.5	7.5	6.2	7.6	5.7	7.7	5.6	7.6	5.5	7.5	5.5	
Exchange rate (ECU/$) (+ = devaluation)	−5.9	−0.9	−1.0	4.0	−1.0	−1.0	−1.0	−1.0	−1.0	−1.0	−1.0	−1.0	−1.0	−1.7	−0.3
Consumption price deflator	2.8	2.9	3.0	2.6	3.2	2.1	3.4	2.1	3.1	2.0	3.0	2.1	3.0	2.0	3.1	2.3
Real private consumption	3.5	3.4	3.0	3.2	2.6	4.2	2.4	4.5	2.5	3.7	2.5	3.6	2.5	3.5	2.7	3.7
Real private investment	5.0	5.7	5.4	7.4	5.1	8.8	4.9	8.7	4.8	8.9	4.8	8.1	4.8	7.3	5.0	7.8
Real total investment	4.6	8.3	4.9	9.9	4.6	8.5	4.5	7.0	4.4	6.1	4.4	4.8	4.4	5.0	4.5	7.1
Real exports (goods + services)	4.2	5.5	4.5	5.8	4.6	6.1	4.6	5.6	4.6	5.5	4.5	5.5	4.5	5.5	4.5	5.6
Real imports (goods + services)	5.9	6.0	5.6	5.7	5.1	6.2	4.7	6.6	4.6	5.8	4.5	5.5	4.5	5.5	5.0	5.9
Fixed capital stock	2.6	2.9	2.8	3.3	3.0	3.9	3.0	3.9	3.0	3.9	3.0	3.6	3.0	3.5	2.9	3.6
Consumption share in GDP (%)	62.4	61.4	62.4	60.7	62.4	60.6	62.4	60.8	62.4	60.8	62.4	60.8	62.4	60.8	
Public investment share in GDP (%)	2.7	3.2	2.6	3.8	2.6	3.9	2.6	3.7	2.6	3.3	2.5	2.7	2.5	2.3	
Total investment share in GDP (%)	20.0	20.5	20.5	21.6	20.9	22.5	21.3	23.1	21.7	23.6	22.1	23.9	22.5	24.3	
Wage share in value added	73.0	70.4	72.7	68.7	72.7	68.6	72.8	68.8	72.7	68.8	72.6	68.8	72.6	68.6	
Gross operating surplus share in value added	27.0	29.6	27.3	31.3	27.3	31.4	27.2	31.2	27.3	31.2	27.4	31.2	27.4	31.4	

a. Yearly rates of growth and averages, except when indicated otherwise.

Table B.9
Labor market statistics for the baseline projection and scenario for the European Community (ten countries)[a]

Component	Year 1	Year 7 Baseline	Year 7 Scenario
Population of working age (15–64 years) (millions of people)	184.4	185.6	185.6
Total active population (millions of people)	120.9	123.4	131.7
Civilian active population (millions of people)	119.3	121.8	130.1
Total employment (millions of people)	108.4	113.0	125.9
Unemployment (line 2 minus line 4) (millions of people)	12.5	10.3	5.8
Unemployment rate (line 5 as a percentage of line 3)	10.5	8.5	4.5

a. Year 1 statistics correspond to the situation in the European Community (ten member states) in 1986.

(The results of the scenario for the labor market are given in more detail in table B.9).

With respect to real wages and productivity, the dynamics of the model simulation are not yet fully stabilized by the seventh year. From further investigations it appears that the equilibrium (steady-state) solution would be a return to a 2.0% rate of growth of both real wages and productivity, with an equilibrium rate of growth of 1.5% for labor demand, when full employment is reached. However, the major problem then becomes (around the tenth year and beyond) one of labor supply shortage. Given the weak demographic growth of the labor force in Europe by then, the labor demand could only be met by further increases in participation rates toward the high levels seen, for example, in Sweden (where the participation rate is currently around 80%, compared to 71% for the European Community at the end of the simulation period).

On the monetary side the real rate of interest (as for the rate of growth of output and the fixed capital stock) stabilizes at 3.5%. This may be compared with a rough estimate of the net real return on capital, measured by the ratio of net operating surplus to capital stock. The equilibrium level of this ratio in the simulation turns out to be about 4%. Given the imprecision in the basis data, this level is quite compatible with the real interest rate. Both remain constant, as do the capital output and capital-to-labor ratio when labor is measured in efficiency units (this supposes that the 2.0% growth in productivity may be assimilated to Harrod-neutral labor-augmenting technical progress).

The model therefore seems to converge to a standard steady-state growth picture with similar growth rates for output, labor (in efficiency units), the capital stock, and the real return on capital. In addition, real wage incomes are growing at the end of the period at the same rate as productivity.

Finally, the expansion of domestic demand and the deterioration in the terms of trade lead to a deterioration of the current balance, which reaches a maximum of 1% of GDP in the fifth year and begins to recover afterward. This deficit is for a substantial part due to net transfer payments (overseas aid, etc.). The trade balance (on goods and services) is in deficit in the middle of the simulation period but returns to equilibrium by the seventh year.

References

Akerlof, G., and J. Yellen. Forthcoming. *Efficiency Wage Models of the Labor Market.* Cambridge: Cambridge University Press.

Albert, M. 1983. *Un pari pour l'Europe.* Paris: Seuil.

Aldrich, J. 1982. "The earnings replacement rate of old-age benefits in twelve countries, 1969–1980." *Social Security Bulletin* 45(4):3–11.

Amano, A., A. Yasahura, F. Hida, and M. Akaike. 1983. "Exchange rate determination in the EMS: An econometric model." EPA Discussion Paper 23. Tokyo: Economic Planning Agency, March.

Barro, R. 1984. *Macroeconomics.* New York: Wiley.

Bean, C., R. Layard, and S. Nickell, eds. 1986. "The rise in unemployment: A multi-country study." *Economica*, supp., 53(210S):S1–S22

Blanchard, O., and L. Summers. 1986a. "Hysteresis and the European unemployment problem," in *NBER Macroeconomics Annual*, S. Fischer, ed. Cambridge, Mass.: National Bureau of Economic Research.

Blanchard, O., and L. Summers. 1986b. "Fiscal increasing returns, hysteresis, real wages, and unemployment." NBER Working Paper 2034. Cambridge, Mass.: National Bureau of Economic Research.

Blanchard, O., R. Dornbusch, J. Drèze, H. Giersch, R. Layard, and M. Monti. 1985. *Employment and Growth in Europe: A Two-Handed Approach.* Brussels: Centre for European Policy Studies.

Boyer, R. 1985. *Flexibilités des marches de travail: Et/ou recherche d'un nouveau rapport salarial.* Paris: CEPREMAT, September.

Bruno, M. 1986. "Aggregate supply and demand factors in OECD unemployment: An update." *Economica*, supp., 53(210S):S35–S52

Bruno, M., and J. Sachs. 1985. *The Economics of Worldwide Stagflation*. Cambridge, Mass.: Harvard University Press.

Bryant, R., D. Henderson, G. Holtham, P. Hooper, and S. Symansky, eds. Forthcoming. *Empirical Macroeconomics for Interdependent Economies: Where Do We Stand?* Washington, D.C.: Brookings Institution.

Bulow, J., and L. Summers. 1985. "A theory of dual labor markets with application to industrial policy, discrimination and Keynesian unemployment." NBER Working Paper 1666. Cambridge, Mass.: National Bureau of Economic Research, October.

Bureau of Labor Statistics. 1985. "Industrial disputes, workers involved and work-time lost in fourteen countries." Washington, D.C.: Department of Labor. Unpublished data.

Bureau of Labor Statistics. 1986. *Employment and Earnings*. Washington, D.C.: Government Printing Office.

Calmfors, L., ed. 1985a. "Proceedings of a conference on trade unions, wage formation and macroeconomic stability." *Scandinavian Journal of Economics* 87(2).

Calmfors, L. 1985b. "The roles of stabilization policy and wage setting for macroeconomic stability: The experience of economies with centralized bargaining." *Kyklos* 38(3):329–347.

Carrol, J., and G. Tamburi. 1985. "Early retirement practices in selected countries." International Labor Office, Geneva. Mimeo.

Clark, K., and L. Summers. 1979. "Unemployment insurance and labor market transactions." *Brookings Papers on Economic Activity* 1:279–323.

Coe, D. 1985. "Nominal wages, the NAIRU and wage flexibility." OECD Economic Studies 5. Paris: OECD, Autumn.

Commission of the European Communities. 1985. "Annual economic report: A cooperative strategy for employment growth." *European Economy* 26:3–154.

Commission of the European Communities. 1986a. "Annual economic report." *European Economy* 30:5–107.

Commission of the European Communities. 1986b. "Results of business surveys on labor market flexibility." *European Economy* 27:5–110.

Commission of the European Communities (Eurostat). 1985a. *ESSPROS: European System of Social Protection Statistics.* Luxembourg: Statistical Office of the European Community.

Commission of the European Communities (Eurostat). 1985b. *Labour force sample surveys, 1983.* Luxembourg: Office of Publications of the European Community.

Crouch, C. 1984. "The conditions for trade union wage restraint," in *The Politics of Inflation and Economic Stagflation,* L. Lindberg and C. Maier, eds. Washington, D.C.: Brookings Institution, 105−148

Davis, K., and D. Rowland. 1983. "Uninsured and undeserved: Inequities in health care in the United States." *Health and Society* 61(2): 149−176.

Dornbusch, R., and S. Fischer. 1981. *Macroeconomics.* New York: McGraw Hill.

Dramais, A. 1986. "COMPACT: A prototype macroeconomic model of the European Community in the world economy." *European Economy* 27:111−160.

Drèze, J. 1986. "Underemployment equilibria: From theory to econometrics and policy." CORE Discussion Paper 8634. Louvain-la-Neuve: CORE.

Emerson, M. 1987. "Regulation or deregulation of the labor market: Policy regimes for the recruitment and dismissal of employees." Economic Paper 54. Brussels: Commission of the European Communities.

European Industrial Relations Review. 1986. *Minimum pay in twelve countries.* Vol. 1. *Adults.* Vol. 2. *Young Workers.* London: European Industrial Relations Review.

Flanagan, R., D. Soskice, and L. Ullman. 1983. *Unionism, Economic Stabilization and Incomes Policies: The European Experience.* Washington: D.C.: Brookings Institution.

Friedman, M. 1968. *Dollars and Deficits.* Englewood Cliffs, N.J.: Prentice Hall.

Hall, R., and J. Taylor. 1985. *Macroeconomics: Theory, Performance and Policy.* New York: Norton.

Halter, W., and R. Hemming. 1985. "Social security financing in the context of demographic change." Paper presented at the Joint Japanese/OECD Conference on Health and Pensions, Paris.

Harrison, B., C. Tilly, and B. Bluestone. 1986. "The great U-turn: Increasing inequity in wage and salary income in the United States." Massachusetts Institute of Technology, Cambridge, Mass. Mimeo.

Hart, R. 1984. *The Economics of Non-Wage Labor Costs*. London: Allen & Unwin.

Haveman, R., V. Halberstadt, and R. Burkhauser, eds. 1984. *Public Policy toward Disabled Workers: Cross-National Analysis of Economic Impacts*. Ithaca, N.Y.: Cornell University Press.

International Employers' Organisation. 1985. *Adapting the Labour Market*. Geneva: International Employers' Organisation, September.

Katz, L. 1986. "Efficiency wage theories: A partial evaluation." NBER Working Paper 1906. Cambridge, Mass.: National Bureau of Economic Research.

Katzenstein, P. 1983. "The smaller European states in the international economy: Economic dependence and corporatist policies," in *The Antinomies of Interdependence*, J. G. Ruggie, ed. New York: Columbia University Press, 91–130.

Layard, R., S. Nickell, and R. Jackman. 1985. "European unemployment is Keynesian and classical but not structural." Working Document 13. Brussels: Centre for European Policy Studies, June.

Layard, R., G. Basevi, O. Blanchard, W. Buiter, and R. Dornbusch. 1984. *Europe: The Case for Unsustainable Growth*. Brussels: Centre for European Policy Studies.

Lehmbruch, G., and P. Schmitte. 1982. *Patterns of Corporatist Policy-Making*. London: Sage.

Leibenstein, H. 1976. *Beyond Economic Man*. Cambridge, Mass.: Harvard University Press.

Malinvaud, E. 1981–1982. *Theorie macroeconomique*, 2 vols. Paris: Dunod.

Meade, J. 1982. *Stagflation*. Vol. 1. *Wage Fixing*. London: Allen & Unwin.

Minford, P. 1983. *Unemployment: Cause and Cure*. London: Martin Robertson.

"Minimum wage in Japan." 1985. *Japanese Ministry of Labor Journal*. November.

Mortensen, J. 1984. "Profitability, relative factor prices and capital/labour substitution in the Community, the United States, and Japan, 1960–1983." *European Economy* 20:29–67.

Nathan, R., and F. Doolittle. 1983. *The Consequences of Cuts: The Effects of the Reagan Domestic Program in State and Local Government*. Princeton, N.J.: Princeton Urban and Regional Research Center.

National Center for Education Statistics. 1985. *The Condition of Education*. Washington, D.C.: US Department of Education.

OECD. 1985a. *Measuring Health Care, 1960–1983: Expenditure, Costs and Performance*. Paris: OECD.

OECD. 1985b. *OECD Employment Outlook*. Paris: OECD.

OECD. 1985c. *Social Expenditure 1960–1990: Problems of Growth and Control*. Paris: OECD.

OECD. 1986a. *Labour Market Flexibility*. Paris: OECD.

OECD. 1986b. "Public pension schemes: Problems of development." Working Paper. Paris: OECD.

O'Higgins, M., G. Schmaus, and G. Stephenson. 1985. *Income Distribution and Redistribution: A Microdata Analysis for Seven Countries*. Luxembourg: Centre d'Etudes de Populations, de Pauvreté et de Politiques Socio-Economiques.

Okun, A. 1975. *Equality and Efficiency: The Great Trade-Off*. Washington, D.C. Brookings Institution.

Ouchi, W. 1981. *Theory Z: How American Business Can Beat the Japanese Challenge*. New York: Avon.

Palmer, J., and J. Sawhill. 1984. *The Reagan Record: An Assessment of America's Changing Domestic Priorities*. New York: Ballinger.

Pechman, J. 1986. *The Rich, the Poor, and the Taxes They Pay*. London: Wheatsheaf.

Piore, M. 1986. "Perspectives on labor market flexibility." *Industrial Relations* 25(2):146–166.

Piore, M., and C. Sabel. 1984. *The Second Industrial Divide: Possibilities for Prosperity*. New York: Basic Books.

Rainwater, L., M. Rein, and J. Schwartz, 1986. *Income Packaging in the Welfare State*. Oxford: Oxford University Press.

Rosen, S. 1985. "Implicit contracts: A survey." *Journal of Economic Literature* 22(3):1144–1174.

Sachs, J. 1985. "High unemployment in Europe: Diagnosis and policy implications." Paper presented at Swedish Employers Organization (SAF) Seminar on Unemployment, Yxtaholm, Sweden, September.

Sachs, J., and W. McKibben. 1985. "Macroeconomic adjustment in the OECD and LDC adjustment." Brookings Discussion Papers. Washington, D.C.: Brookings Institution, February.

Sachs, J., and C. Wyplosz. 1986. "The economic consequences of President Mitterand." *Economic Policy*, spring, 2:262–322.

Schmitte, P., and G. Lehmbruch. 1979. *Trends toward Corporatist Intermediation*. London: Sage.

Smeeding, T., R. Hauser, M. Rainwater, M. Rein, and G. Schaber. 1985. *Poverty in Major Industrialised Countries*. Luxembourg: Centre d'Etudes de Populations, de Pauvreté et de Politiques Socio-Economiques.

Sneessens, H. 1983. "Keynesian versus classical unemployment in Western countries: An attempt at evaluation." University of Louvain-la-Neuve, Louvain-la-Neuve, Belgium. Unpublished.

Sneessens, H., and J. Drèze. 1986. "A discussion of Belgian unemployment combining traditional concepts and disequilibrium econometrics." *Economica* 53:S89–S120

Stiglitz, J. 1984. "Theories of wage rigidity." NBER Working Paper 1442. Cambridge, Mass.: National Bureau of Economic Research, September.

Taylor, J. Forthcoming. "The treatment of expectations in large multi-country econometric models," in *Empirical Macroeconomics for Interdependent Economies*, R. Bryant, D. Henderson, G. Holtham, P. Hooper, and S. Symansky, eds. Washington, D.C.: Brookings Institution.

Thurow, L. 1985a. "A general tendency towards inequality." Department of Economics, Massachusetts Institute of Technology. Unpublished.

Thurow, L. 1985b. *The Management Challenge: Japanese Views*. Cambridge, Mass.: MIT Press.

Thurow, L. 1985c. *The Zero-Sum Solution*. New York: Simon & Schuster.

United States Department of Health and Human Services. 1985 and earlier biennial issues. *Social Security Programs throughout the World.* Washington, D.C.: Government Printing Office.

Vines, D., J. Maciejowoski, and J. Meade. 1983. *Stagflation.* Vol. 2. *Demand Management.* London: Allen & Unwin.

Vitali, L. 1984. "Disability policy in Italy," in *Public Policy Toward Disabled Workers*, R. Haveman, V. Halberstadt, and R. Burkhauser, eds. Ithaca, N.Y.: Cornell University Press, 346–398.

Weisskopf, T. 1985. "Class conflict or class harmony: A study of the effects of worker security on productivity growth in eight advanced countries." University of Michigan, Ann Arbor. Mimeo.

Weitzman, M. 1984. *The Share Economy: Conquering Stagflation.* Cambridge, Mass.: Harvard University Press.

Weitzman, M. 1985. "The Japanese bonus: Profit share or disguised bonus." Department of Economics Working Paper 392. Cambridge, Mass.: Massachusetts Institute of Technology, October.

Yates, S. 1986. "Computerized synthesis of responses to questionnare." *International Research Conference on Social Security Disability Programs.* New Brunswick, N.J.: Bureau of Economic Research, Rutgers University.

Index

Page numbers in *italics* indicate tables.

Austria, benefits in, 1961–1985, *109*

Belgium, benefits in, 1961–1985, *103*

CES. *See* Constant elasticity of substitution
Commission of the European Communities, 37
COMPACT
  aggregate supply and demand conditions, 119–121
  devaluation, 127, *129*
  employment-creating growth strategy, 132–135, *134*
  government sector, 121
  main results of, 135–139, *136, 137, 138*
  monetary and financial relations, 122–123
  monetary expansion, 127, *128*
  prices and incomes, 121
  public investment shock, *124*, 125
  social security contributions, 125–127, *126*
  wage moderation, 127, *130, 131*, 132
Constant elasticity of substitution (CES), 119

Denmark, benefits in, 1961–1985, *105*
Disability benefits, 1985, *93*
Disability pensions, 43–45
Dual labor market model, 10–11

Early retirement pensions, 46–47
Economic model, search for European, 1–4
Education, 57–59
Efficiency models of wage rigidity and employment security
  dual labor market model and, 10–11
  efficiency wage theory and, 9–11
  human resource management and, 11–13
  implicit contract theory and, 11
  labor turnover model and, 10
  shirking model and, 10
  sociological model and, 10
  union threat model and, 10
Efficiency wage theory, 9–11
Employment, theoretical models for, 5–24
  and macroeconomics, 20–24
  neoclassical, 6–8 (*see also* Neoclassical model)
  neocorporatist, 13–20 (*see also* Neocorporatist model)

Employment and social policies, 20–24
  hysteresis hypothesis and, 24
  New-Keynesian approach to, 23–24
Employment protection laws, 32–39
  quotas, 36–37
  reforms in, 38–39
Employment protection regulations, 7
Employment security, 8–13. *See also* Efficiency models of wage rigidity and employment security

Finland, benefits in, 1961–1985, *106*
France, benefits in, 1961–1985, *98*

Germany, benefits in, 1961–1985, *99*
Greece, benefits in, 1961–1985, *113*

Health care, 53, 55–57
Health care benefits, 1985, *95*
High employment
  return to, 73–87
  summary of, in European Community, *79*
Human resource management, 11–13

Implicit contract theory, 11
Income maintenance, 39–52
  disability pensions, *43–45*
  early retirement pensions, 46–47
  maternity benefits, *48–49*
  in 1985, *94*
  reforms in, 50–52
  sickness benefits, *41–42*
  unemployment compensation, 40–41
Income redistribution, 65–71
  changes in, *70*
International Employer's Organisation, 37
Ireland, benefits in, 1961–1985, *111*
Italy, benefits in, 1961–1985, *100*

Japan, benefits in, 1961–1985, *97*

Labor turnover model, 10
Low-employment
  breaking cycle of, 77–84
  origins of, 73–77
  pensions and, 74, 84
  and public expenditure on social programs, 76
  social security tax cuts and, 81–82
  wages and, 83
Luxembourg Income Study, 66

Macroeconomics, 20–24
  hysteresis hypothesis and, 24
  New-Keynesian approach to, 23–24
Maternity benefits, *48–49*
  in 1985, *91*
Minimum wage laws, 27–30
  Japanese, 29
  subminimum for youth, 28
Minimum wage legislation, 7–8
"Misery index," and neocorporatist model, 19–20

Natural rate of unemployment, 6
Neoclassical model, 6–8
  employment protection regulations and, 7
  minimum wage legislation and, 7–8
  natural rate of unemployment and, 6
  policy agenda for, 8
  unemployment compensation and, 7
  wage levels and, 6–7
Neocorporatist model, 13–20
  cost of, 15–16
  defined, 14
  "misery index" and, 19–20
  social security and, 18–19
  strength of, in Western countries, 16–18

Netherlands, benefits in, 1961–1985, *104*
Norway, benefits in, 1961–1985, *107*

Pay systems, 25–32
  bonus payments, 26–27
  centralization of, 28–30
  decentralization of, 27–28
  flexibility in, 25–32
  minimum wage laws and, 27–30
  reforms in, 30–32
Pension(s), 59–64
  and breaking cycle of low employment, 84
  expenditure projections for, *62*
  and low employment, 74
  percentage share of elderly in total population, *61*
  replacement rates of, *60*
Pension benefits, 1985, *92*
Portugal, benefits in, 1961–1985, *114*
Poverty
  percentage of persons in, *67*
  reduction in, *69*
Public expenditure on social programs, evolution of, *115–116*

Shirking model, 10
Sickness benefits, 41–42
  in 1985, *91*
Single European Act, 2
Social model, search for European, 1–4
Social policies, theoretical models, 5–24
  macroeconomics and, 20–24
  neoclassical, 6–8 (*see also* Neoclassical model)
  neocorporatist, 13–20 (*see also* Neocorporatist model)
Social programs, public expenditure on, *76*
Social security
  contributions to, in 1983, *78*
  and neocorporatist model, 18–19

Social services, 52–65
  education, 57–59
  expenditures for, *54*
  health care, 53, 55–57
  pensions, 59–64
Socioeconomic model, 25–72
  hiring and firing regulations, 32–39
  income maintenance, 39–52
  income redistribution, 65–71
  pay systems, 25–32
  social services, 52–65
Sociological mode, 10
Spain, benefits in, 1961–1985, *112*
Sweden, benefits in, 1961–1985, *108*
Switzerland, benefits in, 1961–1985, *110*

Treaty of Rome, changes in, 2

Unemployment benefits, 1985, *90*
Unemployment compensation, 40–41
  and neoclassical model, 7
Unemployment reduction in European community, model simulation, 117–139. *See also* COMPACT
Union threat model, 10
United Kingdom, benefits in, 1961–1985, *101–102*
United States, benefits in, *96*

Wage levels, 6–7
Wage rigidity
  measures of, 27
  theoretical models of efficiency, 8–13 (*see also* Efficiency models of wage rigidity and employment security)